Dare to Be a Daniel

By
Ellen G. White

TEACH Services, Inc.
P U B L I S H I N G
www.TEACHServices.com • (800) 367-1844

Copyright © 2019 TEACH Services, Inc.
ISBN-13: 978-1-57258-289-7 (Paperback)
Library of Congress Control Number: 2004109732

TEACH Services, Inc.
P U B L I S H I N G
www.TEACHServices.com ● (800) 367-1844

Contents

Dare to Be a Daniel

God's Plan for Israel

Every temporal and every spiritual advantage was given to the Jewish nation, the Lord's chosen people. God himself wrought for them, multiplying them in Egypt, delivering them from bondage, and leading them to the land of Canaan, their promised inheritance.

To the Jewish nation were committed the oracles of God, which were to be as a wall of protection round about them. As his chosen people, the Israelites were to show to the nations of the earth that the law of God's kingdom is holy and just and good. By obedience to this law they were to be brought under the control of their Creator and Redeemer, and made a pure, wise people, whose joy it would be to deal justly, to love mercy, and to walk humbly with their God.

Never were the Israelites to depart from the instruction given them by Christ from the pillar of cloud. God declared that if his people would live by the pure, unselfish principles of his law, and thus fulfill his purpose for them, he would honor them before all the world. "Observe and hear all these words which I command thee," he said, "that it may go well with thee, and with thy children after thee forever, when thou doest that which is good and right in the sight of the Lord thy God. When the Lord thy God shall cut off the nations from before thee, whither thou goest to possess them, and thou succeedest them, and dwellest in their land; take heed to thyself that thou be not snared by following them, after that they be destroyed from before thee; and that thou inquire not after their gods, saying, How did these nations serve their gods?...for even their sons and their daughters they have burnt in the fire to their gods. What thing so ever I command you, observe to do it: thou shalt not add thereto, nor diminish from it."

"Ye shall therefore keep all my statutes, and all my judgments, and do them: that the land, whither I bring you to dwell therein, spew you not out. And ye shall not walk in the manners of the nation, which I cast out before you: for they committed all these things, and therefore I abhorred them. But I have said unto you, Ye shall inherit their land, and I will give it unto you to possess it, a land that floweth with milk and honey: I am the Lord your God, which have separated you from other people."

God specified also the sure result of a disregard for his commandments. "If ye will not harken unto me," he declared, "and will not do all these commandments,…I also will do this unto you; I will…set my face against you, and ye shall be slain before your enemies: they that hate you shall reign over you.… And I will make your cities waste, and bring your sanctuaries unto desolation, and I will not smell the savor of your sweet odors. And I will bring the land into desolation: and your enemies which dwell therein shall be astonished at it. And I will scatter you among the heathen, and will draw out a sword after you: and your land shall be desolate, and your cities waste.…And ye shall perish among the heathen, and the land of your enemies shall eat you up."

With these solemn warnings foretelling the results of disobedience, were given words of encouragement. God declared that even if his people should fail of fulfilling his purpose, he would not forsake them utterly. "If they shall confess their iniquity," he said, "and the iniquity of their fathers, with their trespass which they trespassed against me, and that also they have walked contrary unto me; and that I also have walked contrary unto them, and have brought them into the land of their enemies; if then their uncircumcised hearts be humbled, and they then accept of the punishment of their iniquity: then will I remember my covenant with Jacob, and also my covenant with Isaac, and also my covenant with Abraham will I remember; and I will remember the land....When they be in the land of their enemies, I will not cast them away, neither will I abhor them; to destroy them utterly, and to break my covenant with them: for I am the Lord their God. But I will for their sakes remember the covenant of their ancestors, whom I brought forth out of the land of Egypt in the sight of the heathen, that I might be their God: I am the Lord."

These are some of the prophecies concerning Israel. The special advantages and privileges that God's chosen people enjoyed, made their responsibility greater than that of any other people. By holiness of life, by steadfast loyalty, by faithfulness in the payment of tithes and offerings, by cheerful, devoted service, they were to acknowledge God's sovereignty, and testify in word and deed that they were made better by the favors bestowed upon them. Thus they were to be a light to the surrounding nations, revealing to idolatrous peoples the true God and the glory of his character. —*Youth Instructor*, April 23, 1903

Captivity by the Babylonians

"In the third year of the reign of Jehoiakim king of Judah came Nebuchadnezzar king of Babylon unto Jerusalem, and besieged it. And the Lord gave Jehoiakim king of Judah into his hand, with part of the vessels of the house of God: which he carried into the land of Shinar to the house of his god; and he brought the vessels into the treasure-house of his god."

We also read of other invasions by the Babylonians a few years afterward, the first of which was in the reign of Jehoiachin the son of Jehoiakim:—

"Nebuchadnezzar king of Babylon came up against Jerusalem, and the city was besieged. And Nebuchadnezzar...carried away all Jerusalem, and all the princes, and all the mighty men of valor, even ten thousand captives, and all the craftsmen and smiths: none remained, save the poorest sort of the people of the land. And he carried away Jehoiachin...into captivity from Jerusalem to Babylon.

"The king of Babylon made Mattaniah his father's brother king in his stead, and changed his name to Zedekiah. Zedekiah was twenty and one years old when he began to reign, and he reigned eleven years in Jerusalem....And he did that which was evil in the sight of the Lord, according to all that Jehoiakim had done. For through the anger of the Lord it came to pass in Jerusalem and Judah, until he had cast them out from his presence, that Zedekiah rebelled against the king of Babylon.

"And it came to pass in the ninth year of his reign,...that Nebuchadnezzar king of Babylon came, he, and all his host, against Jerusalem, and pitched against it; and they built forts against it round about. And the city was besieged unto the eleventh year of king Zedekiah....And the city was broken up, and all the men of war fled by night:...and the king went the way toward the plain. And the army of the Chaldees pursued after the king, and overtook him in the plains of Jericho: and all his army were scattered from him. So they took the king, and...carried him to Babylon."

"In...the nineteenth year of king Nebuchadnezzar king of Babylon, came Nebuzar-adan, captain of the guard, a servant of the king of Babylon, unto Jerusalem: and he burnt the house of the Lord, and the king's house, and all the houses of Jerusalem, and every great man's house burnt he with fire. And all the army of the Chaldees, that were with the captain of the guard, brake down the walls of Jerusalem round about. Now the rest of the people that were left in the city, and the fugitives that fell away to the king of Babylon, with the remnant of the multitude, did Nebuzar-adan the captain of the guard carry away. But the captain of the guard left of the poor of the land to be vine-dressers and husbandmen....So Judah was carried away out of their land."

The prophet Nehemiah presents the evil-doings of the Jewish nation as the cause of their calamities. After recounting the Lord's dealings with them, and their oft-repeated rebellion, he declares: "They were disobedient, and rebelled against thee, and cast thy law behind their backs, and slew thy prophets which testified against them to turn them to thee, and they wrought great provocations. Therefore thou deliveredst them into the hand of their enemies."

God made Zion his holy habitation, the joy of the whole earth. But notwithstanding his goodness to his chosen people, they forgot him, and wandered into idolatry. Before their dispersion, repeated warnings came to them; but "they refused to harken, and pulled away the shoulder, and stopped their ears, that they should not hear. Yea, they made their hearts as an adamant stone, lest they should hear the law, and the words which the Lord of hosts hath sent in his Spirit by the former prophets: therefore came a great wrath from the Lord of hosts."

If men refuse to receive the admonitions of the Lord, if they persist in walking contrary to his instruction, he can not deliver them from the sure consequences of their own course. If they place themselves in opposition to his purposes, and forsake the principles of heaven, he permits their enemies to humble them.

Through Huldah the prophetess, God declared concerning the unrepentant nation: "Because they have forsaken me, and have burned incense unto other gods, that they might provoke me to anger with all the works of their hands; therefore my wrath shall be kindled against" Jerusalem.

And what was the result?—"Therefore came a great wrath from the Lord of hosts. Therefore it is come to pass, that as he cried, and they would not hear; so they cried, and I would not hear, saith the Lord of hosts: but I scattered them with a whirlwind among all the nations whom they knew not. Thus the land was desolate after them, that no man passed through nor returned: for they laid the pleasant land desolate."

The children of Israel were taken captive to Babylon because they separated from God; they did not maintain his principles unadulterated with the sentiments of the nations around them. The people who should have been a light amid the surrounding darkness, disregarded the word of the Lord. They lived for themselves, and neglected to do the special work God had appointed them. And because of their failure to fulfil his purpose, he permitted them to be humbled by an idolatrous nation.

The Lord could not work for the prosperity of his people, he could not fulfil his covenant with them, while they were untrue to the principles he had given them to maintain, that they might be kept from the methods and practises of the nations that dishonored him. By their spirit and works the children of Israel misrepresented the righteousness of God's character, and the Lord allowed the Babylonians to take them captive. He left his people to their ways; and in the calamities that befell them the innocent suffered with the guilty. —*Youth Instructor*, May 14, 1903

Early Training of Daniel and His Friends

Among the children of Israel who were taken as captives to Babylon at the beginning of the seventy years' captivity, were Christian patriots, young men who were as true as steel to principle, who would not be corrupted by selfishness, who would honor God at the loss of all things. Upon these loyal and true young men the Lord looked with great pleasure. They had to suffer with the guilty, but in the providence of God this captivity was the means of bringing them to the front. Their example of untarnished integrity, while captives in Babylon, shines with heavenly luster.

Among those who remained true to God after reaching the land of their captivity, the prophet Daniel and his three companions are illustrious examples of what even youth may become when united with the God of wisdom. A brief account of the life of these four Hebrews is left on record for the encouragement of those who are called upon to endure trial and temptation.

After his return from the conquest of the Israelites, King Nebuchadnezzar "spake unto Ashpenaz the master of his eunuchs, that he should bring certain of the children of Israel, and of the king's seed, and of the princes; children in whom was no blemish, but well favored, and skilful in all wisdom, and cunning in knowledge, and understanding science, and such as had ability in them to stand in the king's palace, and whom they might teach the learning and the tongue of the Chaldeans. And the king appointed them a daily provision of the king's meat, and of the wine which he drank: so nourishing them three years, that at the end thereof they might stand before the king. Now among these were of the children of Judah, Daniel, Hananiah, Mishael, and Azariah: unto whom the prince of the eunuchs gave names: for he

7

gave unto Daniel the name of Belteshazzar; and to Hananiah, of Shadrach; and to Mishael, of Meshach; and to Azariah, of Abed-nego."

It was not their own pride or ambition that had brought these young men into the king's court, into companionship with those who neither knew nor feared the true God. They were captives in a strange land, placed there by Infinite Wisdom. Separated from home influences and sacred associations, they sought to acquit themselves creditably, for the honor of their downtrodden people, and for the glory of him whose servants they were. These youth had received a right education in early life, and now they honored the instructors of their childhood. With their habits of self-denial were united earnestness of purpose, diligence, and steadfastness.

The education which these four youth had received in Judea was not after the order of the worldly schools, but according to the purpose and plan of God. The school in which they were educated was not after the order of the schools existing before the destruction of the old world by a flood,—schools in which infidel sentiments prevailed, and in which nature was acknowledged and worshiped above the God of nature. These youth were brought up in homes where they were taught the fear of the Lord.

Daniel's parents trained him in his childhood to habits of strict temperance. They taught him that in every act he must conform to nature's laws; that his eating and drinking had a direct influence upon his physical, mental, and moral nature; that he was accountable to God for all his capabilities; and that by no unwise course should he dwarf or enfeeble his powers. As the result of this teaching, God's law was exalted in his mind and reverenced in his heart.

And such an early education was to Daniel and his three companions the means of their preservation. The lessons learned in their earliest years led them to determine to avoid being corrupted in the courts of Babylon. The truth was truth to them. Its principles were stamped upon their hearts. They understood that with the heart man believeth unto righteousness, and with the mouth confession is made unto salvation. The first and great commandment, "Thou shalt love the Lord thy God with all thy heart, and with all thy soul, and with all thy mind," was truth to them, and it must be obeyed.

In the schools established under God's direction, the fear of the Lord was the foundation of all true education. The knowledge of God had been handed down from generation to generation. In Abel, whom Cain killed, and afterward in Enoch, Seth, Methuselah, Noah, and many others, the Lord had faithful witnesses, just men, who kept his fear before their generation. Their memories were not feeble and treacherous. They had received the words of instruction from Adam, and these they repeated to their children and their children's children. Much important history and truth was expressed in song.

Daniel and his companions were familiar with the lives of Abel, Seth, Enoch, and Noah. They cherished the truths that had been passed down from generation to generation. The image of God was engraved upon the heart. When surrounded by an atmosphere of evil, these youth remained uncorrupted. No power or influence could sway them from the principles they had learned in early life by a study of God's word and works.

Young men and young women, study the history of Daniel and his companions. Their lives should inspire you with a determination to be true to God. You must be either loyal or disloyal to him. Christian integrity is strengthened by serving the Lord faithfully. Uplift the standard on which is inscribed, "The commandments of God, and the faith of Jesus." Make no compromise with evil. The line of demarcation between the obedient and the disobedient must be plain and distinct. Firmly determine to do the Lord's will at all times and in all places. —*Youth Instructor*, May 21, 1903

Daniel's Health Plan

Daniel early gave promise of the remarkable ability developed in later years. He and his three companions who were selected to serve in the court of the king, were of princely birth, and are described as "children in whom was no blemish, but well favored, and skilful in all wisdom, and cunning in knowledge, and understanding science, and such as had ability in them." Perceiving the superior talents of these youthful captives, King Nebuchadnezzar determined to prepare them to fill important positions in his kingdom. That they might be fully qualified for their life at court, according to Oriental custom, they were to be taught the language of the Chaldeans, and to be subjected for three years to a thorough course of both physical and intellectual discipline.

The youth in this school of training were not only to be admitted to the royal palace, but it was provided that they should eat of the food, and drink of the wine, which came from the king's table. In all this the king thought that he was not only showing them great honor, but securing for them the best physical and mental development.

In the food provided for the king's table were swine's flesh and other meats which were pronounced unclean by the law given through Moses, and which the Hebrews had been expressly forbidden to eat. Here Daniel was brought to a severe test. Should he adhere to the divine teaching, offend the king, and probably lose not only his position but his life? or should he disregard the commandment of the Lord, and retain the favor of the king, thus securing great intellectual advantages and the most flattering worldly prospects?

Daniel could have argued that, dependent as he was on the king's favor, and subject to his power, there was no other course for him to pursue than to eat of the king's meat and to drink of his wine. But Daniel and his fellows counseled together. They considered how their physical and mental powers would be affected by the use of wine. The wine, they decided, was a snare. They were acquainted with the history of Nadab and Abihu, the record of whose intemperance had been preserved in the parchments of the Pentateuch. They knew that by the constant use of wine these men had become addicted to the liquor habit, and that they had confused their senses by drinking just before engaging in the sacred service of the sanctuary. In their brain-benumbed state, not being able to discern the difference between the sacred and the common, they had put common fire upon their censers, instead of the sacred fire of the Lord's kindling, and for this sin they had been struck dead.

A second consideration with these youthful captives was the fact that the king, before eating, always asked the blessing of his gods upon the food. A portion of the food, and also of the wine, from his table was set apart as an offering to the false gods whom he worshiped. According to the religious ideas of the day, this act consecrated the whole to the heathen gods. Daniel and his three brethren thought that even if they should not actually partake of the king's bounties, a mere pretense of eating the food or drinking the wine, where such idolatry was practised, would be a denial of their faith. To do this would indeed be to implicate themselves with heathenism, and to dishonor the principles of the law of God.

Daniel did not long hesitate. He decided to stand firm in his integrity, let the result be what it might. He "purposed in his heart that he would not defile himself with the portion of the king's meat, nor with the wine which he drank."

In this decision there was much involved. The Hebrew captives were regarded as slaves, but Daniel and his companions were particularly favored because of their apparent intelligence and their comeliness of person. In making their decision they did not act presumptuously, but revealed a firm love for truth and righteousness. They did not choose to be singular, but they must be, else they would ruin their own characters, set a wrong example for others, and dishonor God.

Among professed Christians today there are many who would decide that Daniel was too particular, and would pronounce him narrow and bigoted. They regard the matter of eating and drinking as of too little consequence to require such a decided choice,—one involving the probable sacrifice of every earthly advantage. But in the day of judgment those who reason thus will find that they turned from God's express requirements, and set up their own opinion as a standard of right and wrong. They will find that what seemed to them unimportant was not so regarded by God. His requirements should be sacredly obeyed. Those who accept and obey one of his precepts because it is convenient to do so, while they reject another because its observance would require a sacrifice, lower the standard of right, and by their example lead others to regard lightly his holy law. A "Thus saith the Lord" is to be our rule in all things. —*Youth Instructor*, June 4, 1903

Daniel was subjected to temptations as severe as any that can assail the youth of today; yet he was true to the religious instruction received in early life. He was surrounded with influences calculated to subvert those who would vacillate between principle and inclination; yet the word of God presents him as a faultless character. Daniel dared not trust to his own moral power. Prayer was to him a necessity. He made God his strength, and in all the transactions of his life, the fear of the Lord was before him.

Daniel possessed the grace of genuine meekness. He was true, firm, and noble. He sought to live in peace with all, but wherever principle was involved, he was as unbending as the lofty cedar. In everything that did not come in collision with his allegiance to God, he was respectful and obedient to those who had authority over him; but he had so high a sense of the claims of God that the requirements of earthly rulers were held subordinate. By no selfish consideration could he be induced to swerve from his duty.

The character of Daniel is presented to the world as a striking example of what God's grace can make of men fallen by nature and corrupted by sin. The record of his noble, self-denying life is an encouragement to our common humanity. From it we may gather strength nobly to resist temptation, and firmly, and in the grace of meekness, to stand for the right under the severest trial.

Daniel might have found a plausible excuse to depart from his strictly temperate habits; but the approval of God was dearer to him than the favor of the most powerful earthly potentate,—dearer even than life itself. Having by his courteous conduct obtained favor with Melzar, the officer in charge of the Hebrew youth, Daniel made a request that they might not eat of the king's meat, or drink of his wine. Melzar feared that by complying with this request, he might incur the displeasure of the king; and thus endanger his own life. Like many at the present day, he thought that an abstemious diet would render these youth pale and sickly in appearance, and deficient in muscular strength, while the luxurious food from the king's table would make them ruddy and beautiful, and would promote physical and mental activity.

Daniel requested that the matter be decided by a ten days' trial, the Hebrew youth during this time being supplied with simple food, while their companions ate of the king's dainties. The request was granted, and Daniel felt assured that he had gained his case. Although but a youth, he had seen the injurious effects of wine and luxurious living upon physical and mental health.

At the end of the ten days the result was found to be quite the opposite of Melzar's expectations. Not only in personal appearance, but in physical activity and mental vigor, those who had been temperate in their habits showed a marked superiority over their companions who had indulged appetite. As a result of this trial, Daniel and his associates were permitted to continue their simple diet during the whole course of their training for the duties of the kingdom.

The Lord regarded with approval the firmness and self-denial of these Hebrew youth, and his blessing attended them. He "gave them knowledge and skill in all learning and wisdom: and Daniel had understanding in all visions and dreams." At the expiration of the three years of training, when their ability and acquirements were tested by the king, he "found none like Daniel, Hananiah, Mishael, and Azariah: therefore stood they before the king. And in all matters of wisdom and understanding, that the king inquired of them, he found them ten times better than all the magicians and astrologers that were in all his realm."

The life of Daniel is an inspired illustration of what constitutes a sanctified character. It presents a lesson for all, and especially for the young. A strict compliance with the requirements of God is beneficial to the health of the body and the mind. In order to reach the highest standard of moral and intellectual attainments, it is necessary to seek wisdom and strength from God, and to observe strict temperance in all the habits of life. In the experience of Daniel and his companions we have an instance of the triumph of principle over temptation to indulge the appetite. It shows us that through religious principle young men may triumph over the lusts of the flesh, and remain true to God's requirements, even though it costs them a great sacrifice.

What if Daniel and his companions had made a compromise with those heathen officers, and had yielded to the pressure of the occasion, by eating and drinking as was customary with the Babylonians? That single instance of departure from principle would have weakened their sense of right and their abhorrence of wrong. Indulgence of appetite would have involved the sacrifice of physical vigor, clearness of intellect, and spiritual power. One wrong step would probably have led to others, until, their connection with Heaven being severed, they would have been swept away by temptation.

God has said, "Them that honor me I will honor." While Daniel clung to his God with unwavering trust, the spirit of prophetic power came upon him. While he was instructed of man in the duties of court life, he was taught of God to read the mysteries of future ages, and to present to coming generations, through figures and similitudes, the wonderful things that would come to pass in the last days. —*Youth Instructor*, June 25, 1903

The Call to Temperance

During their three years of training, Daniel and his associates maintained their abstemious habits, their allegiance to God, and their constant dependence upon his power. When the time came for their abilities and acquirements to be tested by the king, they were examined with other candidates for the service of the kingdom. But "among them all was found none like Daniel, Hananiah, Mishael, and Azariah." Their keen apprehension, their choice and exact language, their extensive knowledge, testified to the unimpaired strength and vigor of their mental power. Therefore they stood before the king. "And in all matters of wisdom and understanding, that the king inquired of them, he found them ten times better than all the magicians and astrologers that were in all his realm."

God always honors the right. The most promising youths from all the lands subdued by the great conqueror had been gathered at Babylon, yet amid them all, the Hebrew captives were without a rival. The erect form, the firm, elastic step, the fair countenance, the undimmed senses, the untainted breadth,—all these were insignia of the nobility with which nature honors those who are obedient to her laws.

The lesson here presented is one that we would do well to ponder. A strict compliance with the Bible requirements will be a blessing both to body and soul. The fruit of the Spirit is not only love, joy, and peace, but temperance also. We are enjoined not to defile our bodies; for they are the temples of the Holy Spirit.

The Hebrew captives were men of like passions with ourselves. Amid the seductive influences of the luxurious courts of Babylon, they stood firm. The youth of today are surrounded with allurements to self-indulgence. Especially in our large cities, every form of sensual gratification is made easy and inviting. Those who, like Daniel, refuse to defile themselves, will reap the reward of temperate habits. With their greater physical stamina and increased power of endurance, they have a bank of deposit upon which to draw in case of emergency.

Right physical habits promote mental superiority. Intellectual power, physical stamina, and length of life depend upon immutable laws. Nature's God will not interfere to preserve men from the consequences of violating nature's requirements. He who strives for the mastery must be temperate in all things. Daniel's clearness of mind and firmness of purpose, his power in acquiring knowledge and in resisting temptation, were due in a great degree to the plainness of his diet, in connection with his life of prayer.

There is much sterling truth in the adage, "Every man is the architect of his own fortune." While parents are responsible for the stamp of character, as well as for the education and training, of their sons and daughters, it is still true that our position and usefulness in the world depend, to a great degree, upon our own course of action. Daniel and his companions enjoyed the benefits of correct training and education in early life, but these advantages alone would not have made them what they were. The time came when they must act for themselves,—when their future depended upon their own course. Then they decided to be true to the lessons given them in childhood. The fear of God, which is the beginning of wisdom, was the foundation of their greatness.

The history of Daniel and his youthful companions has been recorded on the pages of the inspired word, for the benefit of the youth of all succeeding ages. Through the record of their fidelity to the principles of temperance, God is speaking today to young men and young women, bidding them gather up the precious rays of light he has given on the subject of Christian temperance, and place themselves in right relation to the laws of health.

There is now need of men who, like Daniel, will do and dare. A pure heart and a strong, fearless hand, are wanted in the world today. God designed that man should be constantly improving, daily reaching a higher point in the scale of excellence. He will help us, if we seek to help ourselves. Our hope of happiness in two worlds depends upon our improvement in one. At every point we should be guarded against the first approach to intemperance.

Dear youth, God calls upon you to do a work which through his grace you can do. "Present your bodies a living sacrifice, holy, acceptable unto God, which is your reasonable service." Stand forth in your God-given manhood and womanhood. Show a purity of tastes, appetite and habits that bears comparison with Daniel's God will reward you with calm nerves, a clear brain, an unimpaired judgment, keen perceptions. The youth of today whose principles are firm and unwavering, will be blessed with health of body, mind, and soul. —*Youth Instructor*, July 9, 1903

The Fight for Temperance

No young man or young woman could be more sorely tempted than were Daniel and his companions. To these four Hebrew youth were apportioned wine and meat from the king's table. But they chose to be temperate. They saw that perils were on every side, and that if they resisted temptation, they must make most decided efforts on their part, and trust the results with God. The youth who desire to stand as Daniel stood must exert their spiritual powers to the very utmost, co-operating with God, and trusting wholly in the strength that he has promised to all who come to him in humble obedience.

There is a constant warfare to be maintained between virtue and vice. The discordant elements of the one, and the pure principles of the other, are at work striving for the mastery. Satan is approaching every soul with some form of temptation on the point of indulgence of appetite. Intemperance is fearfully prevalent. Look where we will, we behold this evil fondly cherished. In spite of the efforts made to control it, intemperance is on the increase. We can not be too earnest in seeking to hinder its progress, to raise the fallen, and to shield the weak from temptation. With our feeble human hands we can do but little, but we have an unfailing Helper. We must not forget that the arm of Christ can reach to the very depths of human woe and degradation. He can give us help to conquer even the terrible demon of intemperance.

There is no class of persons capable of accomplishing more in the warfare against intemperance than are God-fearing youth. In this age the young men in our cities should unite as an army, firmly and decidedly to set themselves against every form of selfish, health-destroying indulgence. What a power they might be for good! How many they might save from becoming demoralized in the halls and gardens fitted up with music and other attractions to allure the youth! Intemperance and profanity and licentiousness are sisters. Let every God-fearing youth gird on the armor and press to the front. Put your names on every temperance pledge presented. Thus you lend your influence in favor of signing the pledge, and induce others to sign it. Let no weak excuse deter you from taking this step. Work for the good of your own souls and for good of others.

The young men and young women who claim to believe the truth for this time can please Jesus only by uniting in an effort to meet the evils that have, with seductive influence, crept in upon society. They should do all they can to stay the tide of intemperance now spreading with demoralizing power over the land. Realizing that intemperance has open, avowed supporters, those who honor God take their position firmly against this tide of evil by which both men and women are being swiftly carried to perdition.

The followers of Jesus will never be ashamed to practise temperance in all things. Then why should any young man blush with shame to refuse the wine-cup or the foaming mug of beer? A refusal to indulge perverted appetite is an honorable act. To sin is unmanly; to indulge in injurious habits of eating and drinking is weak, cowardly, debased; but to deny perverted appetite is strong, brave, noble. In the Babylonian court, Daniel was surrounded by allurements to sin, but by the help of Christ he maintained his integrity. He who can not resist temptation, when every facility for overcoming has been placed within his reach, is not registered in the books of heaven as a man.

Dare to be a Daniel. Dare to stand alone. Have courage to do the right. A cowardly and silent reserve before evil associates, while you listen to their devices, makes you one with them. "Come out from among them, and be ye separate, saith the Lord, and touch not the unclean things; and I will receive you, and will be a Father unto you, and ye shall be my sons and daughters."

At all times and on all occasions it requires moral courage to adhere to the principles of strict temperance. We may expect that by following such a course we shall surprise those who do not totally abstain from all stimulants; but how are we to carry forward the work of reform if we conform to the injurious habits and practises of those with whom we associate?

The holy intelligences of heaven watch the conflict going on between the tempter and the tempted. If the tempted turn from temptation, and in the strength of Jesus conquer, angels rejoice; for Satan has lost in the conflict. In our behalf, Christ, when weakened and suffering on account of hunger, fought the battle against appetite, and conquered Satan. In the name and strength of Jesus every youth may conquer the enemy today on the point of perverted appetite. My dear young friends, advance step by step, until all your habits shall be in harmony with the laws of life and health. He who overcame in the wilderness of temptation declares: "To him that overcometh will I grant to sit with me in my throne, even as I also overcame, and am set down with my Father in his throne."—*Youth Instructor*, July 16, 1903

Ten-Times Wiser

For three years the promising young men whom Nebuchadnezzar, king of Babylon, selected to be trained for filling responsible positions, studied to acquire "the learning and the tongue of the Chaldeans." "At the end of the days...appointed for bringing them in,...the king communed with them; and among them all was found none like Daniel, Hananiah, Mishael, and Azariah: therefore stood they before the king."

True success in any line is not the result of chance, of accident, or of destiny; it is the outworking of God's providence, the reward of faith and discretion, of virtue and persevering labor. In acquiring the wisdom of the Babylonians, Daniel and his three companions were far more successful than their fellow students, but their learning did not come by chance; they obtained knowledge by the faithful use of their powers, under the guidance of the Holy Spirit.

These youth placed themselves in connection with the Source of all wisdom. They made the knowledge of God the foundation of their education. Other young men had the same advantages, but they did not, like the faithful Hebrew youth, bend all their energies to seek wisdom,—the knowledge of God as revealed in his word and works. They did not unite with these youth in searching the portion of the Old Testament then written, and making God's word their highest instructor.

In faith the Hebrew captives prayed for wisdom, and then lived out their own prayers. To this end they avoided everything that would weaken physical or mental power. At the same time, they improved every opportunity given them to become intelligent in all lines of learning. They sought to acquire knowledge for a purpose,—to honor and glorify God. They realized that in order to

22

stand as representatives of true religion amid the false religions of heathenism, they must have clearness of intellect, and must perfect a Christian character.

These youth determined to secure a well-balanced education. They became skilled in secular as well as religious knowledge; but they studied science without being corrupted. While obtaining a knowledge of the sciences, they were studying, also, the highest science that mortals can study,—the science of salvation. They received light direct from the throne of heaven. The Lord himself was their educator. The golden links of the chain of heaven connected the finite with the Infinite. Constantly praying, conscientiously studying, keeping themselves in touch with the Unseen, they walked with God, as did Enoch.

The history of Daniel and his companions contains a lesson for us. Inspiration declares that "the fear of the Lord is the beginning of wisdom." Religious principle lies at the foundation of the highest education. If our youth are but balanced by principle, they may with safety improve the mental powers to the very highest extent, and may take all their attainments with them into the future life. There are many who might become mighty men, if, like these faithful Hebrews, they would learn of Christ, the world's greatest Teacher.

We would not prevent the youth from obtaining knowledge in literature, science, and art; but we would impress upon the minds of all the necessity of first obtaining a knowledge of God and of his will, that the influence of his Spirit may direct every advancement in educational lines.

Daniel placed himself in the channel of heavenly light, where he could commune with God in prayer. God co-operates with the human agencies who place themselves in this channel. Increased light is constantly shining from heaven upon those who seek for divine wisdom. Those who do not choose to place themselves in this channel meet with terrible loss. Students who exalt the sciences above the God of science, will be ignorant when they think themselves wise. Young men, young women, if you can not afford time to pray, can not give time for communion with God, for self-examination, and do not appreciate the wisdom that comes from God alone, all your learning will be defective, and your education will prove a hindrance instead of an advantage.

The lesson that the youth of today most need to learn, is the importance of seeking with all the heart to know God and to obey him implicitly. The science of the salvation of the human soul is the first lesson of life. Every line of literary or scientific knowledge is to be made secondary to this. To know God, and Jesus Christ whom he has sent, is life eternal. —*Youth Instructor*, August 6, 1903

Perseverance

We read that Daniel "purposed in his heart" that he would not eat of the luxuries of the king's table, nor drink of his wines. This purpose was not formed without due reflection and prayer, and when once his position was taken, he was not to be moved from it.

Daniel's companions, also, resolutely purposed to choose the real, the true, and the useful, rather than the momentary indulgence of appetite and pride. They resolved that their God-given talents should not be perverted and enfeebled by selfish indulgence. They reverenced their own manhood. They kept their eyes steadfastly fixed on the good they wished to accomplish. They determined to do all in their power to place themselves in right relation to God; and the Lord was not unmindful of their persevering, earnest effort.

When the four Hebrew youth were receiving an education for the king's court in Babylon, they did not feel that the blessing of the Lord was a substitute for the taxing effort required of them. They were diligent in study; for they discerned that through the grace of God their destiny depended upon their own will and action. They were to bring all their ability to the work; and by close, severe taxation of their powers, they were to make the most of their opportunities for study and labor.

While these youth were working out their own salvation, God was working in them to will and to do of his good pleasure. Here are revealed the conditions of success. To make God's grace our own, we must act our part. The Lord does not propose to perform for us either the willing or the doing. His grace is given to work in us to will and to do, but never as a substitute for our effort. Our souls are to be aroused to co-operate. The Holy Spirit works in us, that we may work out our own salvation. This is the practical lesson the Holy Spirit is striving to teach us. "It is God which worketh in you both to will and to do of his good pleasure."

The Lord will co-operate with all who earnestly strive to be faithful in his service, as he co-operated with Daniel and his three companions. Fine mental qualities and a high tone of moral character are not the result of accident. God gives opportunities; success depends upon the use made of them. The openings of Providence must be quickly discerned and eagerly entered. There are many who might become mighty men, if, like Daniel, they would depend upon God for grace to be overcomers, and for strength and efficiency to do their work.

I address you, young men: Be faithful. Put heart into your work. Imitate none who are slothful, and who give divided service. Actions, often repeated, form habits, habits form character. Patiently perform the little duties of life. So long as you undervalue the importance of faithfulness in the little duties, your character-building will be unsatisfactory. In the sight of Omnipotence, every duty is important. The Lord has said, "He that is faithful in that which is least is faithful also in much." In the life of a true Christian there are no non-essentials.

Many who claim to be Christians are working at cross-purposes with God. Many are waiting for some great work to be brought to them. Daily they lose opportunities for showing their faithfulness to God; daily they fail of discharging with whole-heartedness the little duties of life, which seem to them uninteresting. While waiting for some great work in which they may exercise their supposedly great talents, and thus satisfy their ambitious longings, their life passes away.

My dear young friends, do the work that lies nearest at hand. Turn your attention to some humble line of effort within your reach. Put mind and heart into the doing of this work. Force your thoughts to act intelligently on the things that you can do at home. Thus you will be fitting yourself for greater usefulness. Remember that of King Hezekiah it is written: "In every work that he began,…he did it with all his heart, and prospered."

The ability to fix the thoughts on the work in hand, is a great blessing. God-fearing youth should strive to discharge their duties with thoughtful consideration, keeping the thoughts in the right channel, and doing their best. They should recognize their present duties, and fulfil them without allowing the mind to wander. This kind of mental discipline will be helpful and beneficial throughout life. Those who learn to put thought into everything they undertake, however small the work may appear, will be of use in the world.

Dear youth, be earnest, be persevering. "Gird up the loins of your mind." Stand like Daniel, the faithful Hebrew, who purposed in his heart to be true to God. Do not disappoint your parents and friends. And there is Another to be remembered. Do not disappoint Him who so loved you that he gave his life to make it possible for you to be co-laborers with God.

The desire to honor God should be to us the most powerful of all motives. It should lead us to make every exertion to improve the privileges and opportunities provided for us, that we may understand how to use wisely the Lord's goods. It should lead us to keep brain, bone, muscle, and nerve in the most healthful condition, that our physical strength and mental clearness may make us faithful stewards. Selfish interest, if given room to act, dwarfs the mind, and hardens the heart; if allowed to control, it destroys moral power. Then disappointment comes. The selfish man has divorced himself from God, and sold himself to unworthy pursuits. He can not be happy; for he can not respect himself. He has lowered himself in his own estimation. He is a failure.

True success is given to men and women by the God who gave success to Daniel. He who read the heart of Daniel looked with pleasure upon his servant's purity of motive, his determination to honor the Lord. Those who in their life fulfil God's purpose, must put forth painstaking effort, applying themselves closely and earnestly to the accomplishment of whatever he gives them to do.

Dear reader, will you not determine to be as was Daniel,—a loyal, steadfast servant of the Lord of hosts? The God of Daniel works mightily in behalf of every one who seeks to know and to do his will. By the impartation of his Spirit he strengthens every true purpose, every noble resolution. —*Youth Instructor*, August 20, 1903

Nebuchadnezzar's Dream

In the same year that Daniel and his companions entered the service of the king of Babylon, events occurred that severely tested the integrity of these youthful Hebrews, and revealed to an idolatrous nation the power and faithfulness of the God of Israel.

While King Nebuchadnezzar was looking forward with anxious forebodings to the future, he had a remarkable dream, by which "his spirit was troubled, and his sleep broke from him." Although this vision of the night made a deep impression on his mind, he found it impossible to recall the particulars. He applied to his astrologers and magicians, and with promises of great wealth and honor commanded them to tell him his dream and its interpretation. But they said, "Tell thy servants the dream, and we will show the interpretation."

The Lord in his providence had a wise purpose in view in giving Nebuchadnezzar this dream, and then causing him to forget the particulars, but to retain the fearful impression made upon his mind. The Lord desired to expose the pretensions of the wise men of Babylon. The king knew that if they could tell the interpretation, they could tell the dream as well. Angered over their inability to relieve his mind, he threatened that they should all be slain, if, in a given time, the dream were not made known. "The thing is gone from me," he said to the Chaldeans; "if ye will not make known unto me the dream, with the interpretation thereof, ye shall be cut to pieces, and your houses shall be made a dunghill. But if ye show the dream, and the interpretation thereof, ye shall receive of me gifts and rewards and great honor: therefore show me the dream, and the interpretation thereof." Still the wise men returned the same answer, "Let the king tell his servants the dream, and we will show the interpretation of it."

Nebuchadnezzar began to see that the men whom he trusted to reveal mysteries by means of their boasted wisdom, failed him in his great perplexity, and he said: "I know of a certainty that ye would gain the time, because ye see the thing is gone from me. But if ye will not make known unto me the dream, there is but one decree for you: for ye have prepared lying and corrupt words to speak before me, till the time be changed: therefore tell me the dream, and I shall know that ye can show me the interpretation thereof.

"The Chaldeans answered before the king, and said, There is not a man upon the earth that can show the king's matter: therefore there is no king, lord, nor ruler, that asked such things at any magician, or astrologer, or Chaldean. And it is a rare thing that the king requireth, and there is none other that can show it before the king, except the gods, whose dwelling is not with flesh.

"For this cause the king was angry and very furious, and commanded to destroy all the wise men of Babylon."

When the decree went forth that all the wise men of Babylon should be destroyed, Daniel and his fellows were sought for, and informed that in accordance with the king's command, they must be slain. "Then Daniel answered," not in a spirit of retaliation, but "with counsel and wisdom," "the captain of the king's guard," who "was gone forth to slay the wise men of Babylon." "Why," Daniel inquired, "is the decree so hasty from the king?" Taking his life in his hand, he ventured to enter the king's presence, and begged that time be granted, in order that he might reveal to him the dream and its interpretation. To this request the monarch acceded.

"Then Daniel went to his house, and made the thing known to Hananiah, Mishael, and Azariah, his companions: that they would desire mercies of the God of heaven concerning this secret; that Daniel and his fellows should not perish with the rest of the wise men of Babylon." Together the Hebrew youth presented the matter before God, and sought for wisdom from the Source of light and knowledge. Although for a time they had lived in the king's court, surrounded with temptation, they had not forgotten their responsibility to God. They were strong in the consciousness that His providence had placed them where they were; that they were doing His work, and meeting the demands of duty. They had confidence toward God. In times past they had turned to Him for strength when in perplexity and danger, and He had been to them an ever-present help.

The servants of God did not plead with Him in vain. They had honored Him, and in their hour of trial He honored them. The Spirit of the Lord rested upon Daniel and his fellows, and the secret was revealed to Daniel in a night vision. He hastened to request an interview with the king.

The Jewish captive stood before the monarch of the most powerful empire that the sun ever shone upon. Notwithstanding his riches and glory, Nebuchadnezzar was in great distress of mind, but the youthful exile was calm and happy in his God. Then, if ever, was an opportunity for Daniel to exalt himself—to make prominent his own goodness and superior wisdom. But his first effort was to disclaim all honor for himself, and to exalt God as the Source of wisdom:—

"The secret which the king hath demanded can not the wise men, the astrologers, the magicians, the soothsayers, show unto the king; but there is a God in heaven that revealeth secrets, and maketh known to the king Nebuchadnezzar what shall be in the latter days."

Daniel proceeded to relate the dream. "Thy dream," he declared, "and the visions of thy head upon thy bed, are these; As for thee, O king, thy thoughts came into thy mind upon thy bed, what should come to pass hereafter: and he that revealeth secrets maketh known to thee what shall come to pass. But as for me, this secret is not revealed to me for any wisdom that I have more than any living, but for their sakes that shall make known the interpretation to the king, and that thou mightest know the thoughts of thy heart.

"Thou, O king, sawest, and behold a great image. This great image, whose brightness was excellent, stood before thee; and the form thereof was terrible. This image's head was of fine gold, his breast and arms of silver, his belly and his thighs of brass, his legs of iron, his feet part of iron and part of clay. Thou sawest till that a stone was cut out without hands, which smote the image upon his feet that were of iron and clay and brake them to pieces. Then was the iron, the clay, the brass, the silver, and the gold, broken to pieces together, and became like the chaff of the summer threshing-floors; and the wind carried them away, that no place was found for them: and the stone that smote the image became a great mountain, and filled the whole earth."

Listening with solemn attention as every particular was reproduced, the king recognized this as the dream over which he had been so troubled; and he was prepared to receive with favor the interpretation.—*Youth Instructor*, September 1, 1903

Interpreting Nebuchadnezzar's Dream

Having described the image that the king had seen, Daniel gave the interpretation, foretelling the remarkable events that were to take place in prophetic history:—

"Thou, O king, art a king of kings: for the God of heaven hath given thee a kingdom, power, and strength, and glory. And wheresoever the children of men dwell, the beasts of the field and the fowls of the heaven hath he given into thine hand, and hath made thee ruler over them all. Thou art this head of gold.

"And after thee shall arise another kingdom inferior to thee, and another third kingdom of brass, which shall bear rule over all the earth.

"And the fourth kingdom shall be strong as iron: forasmuch as iron breaketh in pieces and subdueth all things: and as iron that breaketh all these, shall it break in pieces and bruise. And whereas thou sawest the feet and toes, part of potters' clay, and part of iron, the kingdom shall be divided; but there shall be in it of the strength of the iron, forasmuch as thou sawest the iron mixed with miry clay. And as the toes of the feet were part of iron, and part of clay, so the kingdom shall be partly strong, and partly broken. And whereas thou sawest iron mixed with miry clay, they shall mingle themselves with the seed of men: but they shall not cleave one to another, even as iron is not mixed with clay.

"And in the days of these kings shall the God of heaven set up a kingdom, which shall never be destroyed: and the kingdom shall not be left to other people, but it shall break in pieces and consume all these kingdoms, and it shall stand forever. Forasmuch as thou sawest that the stone was cut out of the mountain without hands, and that it brake in pieces the iron, the brass, the clay, the silver and the gold; the great God hath made known to

33

the king what shall come to pass hereafter: and the dream is certain, and the interpretation thereof sure."

Nebuchadnezzar felt that he could accept this interpretation as a divine revelation; for to Daniel had been revealed every detail of the dream. The solemn truths conveyed by the interpretation of this vision of the night made a deep impression on the sovereign's mind, and in humility and awe he "fell upon his face, and worshiped," saying, "Of a truth it is, that your God is a God of gods, and a Lord of kings, and a revealer of secrets, seeing thou couldest reveal this secret."

Daniel's exposition of this dream resulted in the king's conferring honor and dignity upon him and his companions. "The king made Daniel a great man, and gave him many great gifts, and made him ruler over the whole province of Babylon, and chief of the governors over all the wise men of Babylon. Then Daniel requested of the king, and he set Shadrach, Meshach, and Abed-nego, over the affairs of the province of Babylon: but Daniel sat in the gate of the king." "The gate of the king" was a place where justice was dispensed. Daniel's three companions were made counselors, judges, and rulers in the land. These men were not puffed up with vanity, but they saw and rejoiced that God was recognized above all earthly potentates, and that his kingdom was extolled above all earthly kingdoms.

The Lord was working in the Babylonian kingdom, and communicating light to the four Hebrew youth, in order that he might represent his work before the idolatrous nation. He would reveal that he had power over the kingdoms of the world,—power to enthrone and to dethrone kings. The King over all kings was communicating great truths to the Babylonian monarch, and awakening in his mind a realization of his responsibility to God. Nebuchadnezzar saw clearly the difference between the wisdom of God and the wisdom of the most learned men of his kingdom.

The events of the future, reaching down to the end of time, were opened before the king of Babylon, in order that he might have light on this important subject. The record of the dream and its interpretation was traced by the prophetic pen, in order that the rulers of the kingdoms that should succeed Babylon might have the same light. —*Youth Instructor*, September 8, 1903

Deterioration From Within

"Righteousness exalteth a nation: but sin is a reproach to any people."

The image revealed to Nebuchadnezzar, while representing the deterioration of the kingdoms of the earth in power and glory, also fitly represents the deterioration of religion and morality among the people of these kingdoms. As nations forget God, in like proportion they become weak morally.

Babylon passed away because in her prosperity she forgot God, and ascribed the glory of her prosperity to human achievement.

The Medo-Persian kingdom was visited by the wrath of heaven because in this kingdom God's law was trampled under foot. The fear of the Lord found no place in the hearts of the people. The prevailing influences in Medo-Persia were wickedness, blasphemy, and corruption.

The kingdoms that followed were even more base and corrupt. They deteriorated because they cast off their allegiance to God. As they forgot him, they sank lower and still lower in the scale of moral value.

The vast empire of Rome crumbled to pieces, and from its ruins rose that mighty power, the Roman Catholic Church. This church boasts of her infallibility and her hereditary religion. But this religion is a horror to all who are acquainted with the secrets of the mystery of iniquity. The priests of this church maintain their ascendency by keeping the people in ignorance of God's will, as revealed in the Scriptures.

It is sin that is ruining nations today. Even many leaders in the religious world have not a good conscience toward God. Many of those who claim to be Protestants have not the faith in God's word that Luther had in the early days of the Reformation. They have left the old landmarks, and depend on ceremony and formal display to make up for their lack of the purity and piety, the meekness and lowliness, found in obedience to God.

There is no real standard of righteousness apart from God's law. By obedience to this law the intellect is strengthened, and the conscience is enlightened and made sensitive. The youth need to gain a clear understanding of God's law. They are not left to follow blindly the guidance of men. The great prophetic waymarks which God himself has set up show the path of obedience to be the only path that can be followed with certainty.

Those who love and obey the law of God will meet with trials and temptations; but if they hope and pray, and trust his word, they will be able to say, with Paul, "I am persuaded, that neither death, nor life, nor angels, nor principalities, nor powers, nor things present, nor things to come, nor height, nor depth, nor any other creature, shall be able to separate us from the love of God, which is in Christ Jesus our Lord."

My dear young friends, have you wholly given yourselves up to God, to do his will? Are you transformed by the grace of Christ? Some claim to be one with Christ, while their special work is to make void the law of God. Will you accept their assertions? How will you distinguish God's true servants from the false prophets that Christ said would arise to deceive many? There is only one test of character,—God's holy law.

We are living in a momentous period of this earth's history. The final conflict is just before us. We see the world corrupted under the inhabitants thereof. Satanic agencies have made the earth a stage for horrors that no language can describe. War and bloodshed are carried on by nations claiming to be Christian. A disregard for God's law has brought the sure result.

"We wrestle not against flesh and blood, but against principalities, against powers, against the rulers of the darkness of this world, against spiritual wickedness in high places. Wherefore

37

take unto you the whole armor of God, that ye may be able to withstand in the evil day, and having done all, to stand." "Be strong in the Lord, and in the power of his might. Put on the whole armor of God, that ye may be able to stand against the wiles of the devil."

There will be a sharp conflict between those who are loyal to God and those who cast scorn upon his law. The church has joined hands with the world. Reverence for God's law has been subverted. The religious leaders have taught for doctrine the commandments of men. As it was in the days of Noah, so it is in this age. But shall the prevalence of disloyalty and transgression cause those who have reverenced God's law to have less respect for it, or to unite with the powers of earth in attempting to make it void?

The test comes to every one. There are only two sides. Dear young reader, on which side are you standing? —*Youth Instructor*, September 22, 1903

Obedience—The Mark of a Disciple

The strength of nations and of individuals is not found in the opportunities and facilities that appear to make them invincible; it is not found in their boasted greatness. That which alone can make them great or strong is the power of God. They themselves, by their attitude toward his purpose, decide their own destiny.

Human histories relate man's achievements, his victories in battle, his success in attaining worldly greatness. God's history describes man as heaven views him. In the divine records all his merit is seen to consist in his obedience to God's requirements. His disobedience is faithfully chronicled as meriting the punishment he will surely receive. In the light of eternity it will be seen that God deals with men in accordance with the momentous question of obedience or disobedience.

Hundreds of years before certain nations came upon the stage of action, the Omniscient One looked down the ages, and predicted through his servants the prophets the rise and fall of the universal kingdoms. The prophet Daniel, when interpreting to the king of Babylon the dream of the great image,—an image symbolic of the kingdoms of the world,—declared to Nebuchadnezzar that his kingdom should be superseded. His greatness and power in God's world would have their day, and a second kingdom would arise, which also would have its period of trial as to whether it would exalt the one Ruler, the only true God. Not doing this, its glory would fade away, and a third kingdom would occupy its place. Proved by obedience or disobedience, this also would pass away; and a fourth, strong as iron, would subdue the nations of the world. These predictions of the Infinite One, recorded on the prophetic page and traced on the pages of history, were given to demonstrate that God is the ruling power in the affairs of this world. He changes the times and the seasons, he removes kings and sets up kings, to fulfil his own purpose.

Under King Nebuchadnezzar, Babylon was the richest and most powerful kingdom on the earth. Its riches and splendor have been faintly portrayed by Inspiration. But it did not fulfil God's purpose; and when his time had come, this kingdom of pride and power, ruled by men of the highest intellect, was broken, shattered, helpless. Christ has declared, "Without me ye can do nothing." The illustrious statesmen of Babylon did not regard themselves as dependent on God. They thought that they had created all their grandeur and exaltation. But when God spoke, they were as the grass that withereth, and the flower of the grass that fadeth away. The word and will of God alone endure forever.

If these several kingdoms had kept the fear of the Lord always before them, they would have been given wisdom and power, which would have bound them together and kept them strong. But the rulers of the kingdoms of the world made God their strength only when harassed and perplexed. Failing to obtain help from their great men, they sought it from men like Daniel, men who they knew honored the living God and were honored by him. To these men they appealed to unravel for them the mysteries of Providence; for they had separated themselves so far from God by transgression that they could not understand his warnings. They were forced to appeal to those whose minds were illuminated by heavenly light, for an explanation of the mysteries they could not comprehend.

The voice of God, heard in past ages, is sounding down along the line, from century to century, through generations that have come upon the stage of action and passed away. Shall God speak, and his voice not be respected? What power mapped out all this history, that nations, one after another, should arise at the predicted time and fill their appointed place, unconsciously witnessing to the truth of that which they themselves knew not the meaning.

The centuries have their mission. Every moment has its work. Each is passing into eternity with its burden, Well done, thou good and faithful servant, or, Woe to the wicked and slothful servant. God is still dealing with earthly kingdoms. He is in the great cities. His eyes behold, his eyelids try, the doings of the children of men. We are not to say, God was, but, God is. He sees the very sparrow's fall, the leaf that falls from the tree, and the king who is dethroned. All are under the control of the Infinite One. Everything is changing. Cities and nations are being measured by the plummet in the hand of God. He never makes a mistake. He reads correctly. Everything earthly is unsettled, but the truth abides forever.

In the eyes of the world, those who serve God may appear weak. They may be apparently sinking beneath the billows, but with the next billow, they are seen rising nearer to their haven. I give unto them eternal life, saith our Lord, and none shall be able to pluck them out of my hand. Though kings shall be cast down, and nations removed, the souls that through faith link themselves with God's purpose shall abide forever. "They that be wise shall shine as the brightness of the firmament; and they that turn many to righteousness as the stars forever and forever." —*Youth Instructor*, September 29, 1903

True Wisdom

The prophetic events related in Nebuchadnezzar's dream were of consequence to him, but the dream was taken from him in order that the wise men should not place upon it a false interpretation. The lessons taught by the dream were given by God for those who live in our day. The inability of the wise men to tell the dream is a representation of the limitations of the wise men of the present day, who, not having wisdom and discernment from the Most High, are unable to understand the prophecies. Although he may be learned in the world's lore, the man who is not listening to hear what the Lord says in his word, and who is not opening his heart to receive this word, that he may give it to others, is not a representative of the God of heaven. Not many great and learned men of the earth will gladly receive the truth unto eternal life, though to all of them the truth will be proclaimed.

Young men and young women may obtain the highest earthly education, and yet may be ignorant of the first principles that would make them subjects of the kingdom of God. Human learning can not qualify any one for the heavenly kingdom. The subjects of Christ's kingdom are not made thus by forms and ceremonies, or by long study of books. "This is life eternal, that they might know thee the only true God, and Jesus Christ, whom thou hast sent." The members of Christ's kingdom are members of his body, of which he himself is the head. They are the elect sons of God, "a royal priesthood, an holy nation, a peculiar people;" that they should show forth the praises of him who has called them out of darkness into his marvelous light.

The Old and the New Testament Scriptures need to be studied daily. The knowledge of God and the wisdom of God come to the student who is a constant learner of his ways and works. The

Bible is to be our light, our educator. When the youth learn to believe that God sends the dew, the rain, and the sunshine from heaven, causing vegetation to flourish; when they realize that all blessings come from him, and that thanksgiving and praise are due to him, they will be led to acknowledge God in all their ways, and discharge with fidelity their duties day by day; God will be in all their thoughts. Then they can trust him for tomorrow, and avoid the anxious care that brings unhappiness into the lives of so many. "Seek ye first the kingdom of God, and his righteousness; and all these things shall be added unto you."

Many young men, in talking about science, are wise above that which is written; they seek to explain, by something that meets their finite comprehension, the ways and work of God; but it is all a miserable failure. True science and Inspiration are in perfect harmony. False science is something independent of God. It is pretentious ignorance.

One of the greatest evils that has attended the quest of knowledge, the investigation of science, is that those who engage in these researches too often lose sight of the divine character of pure and unadulterated religion. The worldly wise have attempted to explain, on scientific principles, the influence of the Spirit of God upon the heart. The least advance in this direction will lead the mind into the mazes of skepticism. The religion of the Bible is simply the mystery of godliness; no human mind can fully understand it, and it is utterly incomprehensible to the unregenerate heart.

The youth will not become weak-minded or inefficient by consecrating themselves to the service of God. To many, education means a knowledge of books; but "the fear of the Lord is the beginning of wisdom." The youngest child who loves and fears God is greater in his sight than the most talented and learned man who neglects the matter of personal salvation. The youth who consecrate their hearts and lives to God are placing themselves in connection with the Fountain of all wisdom and excellence.

If the youth will but learn of the heavenly Teacher, as Daniel did, they will know for themselves that the fear of the Lord is indeed the beginning of wisdom. Having thus laid a sure foundation, they may, like Daniel, turn every privilege and opportunity to the very best account, and may rise to any height in intellectual attainments. Consecrated to God, and having the protection of his grace and the quickening influence of his Holy Spirit, they will manifest deeper intellectual power than the mere worldling.

To learn science through the interpretation that men have placed on it, is to obtain a false education. To learn of God, and of Jesus Christ, whom he has sent, is to learn the science of the Bible. The pure in heart see God in every providence, in every phase of true education. They recognize the first approach of the light that radiates from God's throne. Communications from heaven are made to those who will catch the first gleams of spiritual knowledge.

The students in our schools are to regard the knowledge of God as above everything else. Only by searching the Scriptures can this knowledge be attained. "The preaching of the cross is to them that perish foolishness; but unto us which are saved it is the power of God. For it is written, I will destroy the wisdom of the wise, and will bring to nothing the understanding of the prudent....The foolishness of God is wiser than men; and the weakness of God is stronger than men....But of him are ye in Christ Jesus, who of God is made unto us wisdom, and righteousness, and sanctification, and redemption: that, according as it is written, He that glorieth, let him glory in the Lord." —*Youth Instructor*, November 24, 1903

The Infallible Word

When Nebuchadnezzar's dream of the great image was revealed to Daniel in a night vision, his first act was to thank God for this revelation. "Blessed be the name of God forever and ever," he exclaimed; "for wisdom and might are his: and he changeth the times and the seasons: he removeth kings, and setteth up kings: he giveth wisdom unto the wise, and knowledge to them that know understanding: he revealeth the deep and secret things: he knoweth what is in the darkness, and the light dwelleth with him. I thank thee, and praise thee, O thou God of my fathers, who hast given me wisdom and might, and hast made known unto me now what we desired of thee: for thou hast now made known unto us the king's matter."

In past ages the Lord God of heaven revealed his secrets to his prophets. The present and the future are equally clear to him. The voice of God echoes down the ages, telling man what is to take place. Kings and princes take their places at their appointed time. They think they are carrying out their own purposes, but in reality they are fulfilling the word that God has spoken.

Paul declares that the records of God's dealings with mankind in the past "are written for our admonition, upon whom the ends of the world are come." Daniel's history is given us for our admonition. "The secret of the Lord is with them that fear him." Daniel's God still lives and reigns. He has not closed heaven against his people. As in the Jewish age, so in this age, God reveals his secrets to his servants the prophets.

The apostle Peter says: "We have also a more sure word of prophecy; whereunto ye do well that ye take heed, as unto a light that shineth in a dark place, until the day dawn, and the day-star arise in your hearts: knowing this first, that no prophecy of the Scripture is of any private interpretation. For the prophecy came not in old time by the will of man: but holy men of God spake as they were moved by the Holy Ghost."

The unbelieving and godless do not discern the importance of the signs of the times, foretold in the prophetic word. In ignorance they may refuse to accept the inspired record. But when professed Christians speak sneeringly of the ways and means employed by the great I AM to make his purposes known, they show themselves to be ignorant both of the Scriptures and of the power of God. The Creator knows just what elements he has to deal with in human nature. He knows what means to employ to obtain the desired results.

Man's word fails. He who makes the assertions of men his dependence, may well tremble; for he will some day be as a shipwrecked vessel. God's word is infallible, and endures forever. Christ declares, "Verily I say unto you, Till heaven and earth pass, one jot or one title shall in no wise pass from the law, till all be fulfilled." God's word will endure throughout the ceaseless ages of eternity. —*Youth Instructor*, December 1, 1903

Truth's Counterfeit

The dream of the great image, by which were opened future events reaching to the end of time, was given to Nebuchadnezzar that he might understand the part he was to act in the world's history, and also the relation that his kingdom sustained to the kingdom of heaven. This wonderful dream caused a marked change in his ideas and opinions, and for a little time he was influenced by the fear of God; but his heart was not yet cleansed from its pride, its worldly ambition, its desire for self-exaltation.

The prophet Daniel described to King Nebuchadnezzar the rise and fall of the kingdoms that were to succeed Babylon; but the king did not cherish the conviction that came to his mind in regard to the fall of all earthly governments, and the greatness and power of Jehovah's kingdom. After the first impression wore away, he thought only of his own greatness, and studied how the dream might be turned to his own honor.

The words, "Thou art this head of gold," made the deepest impression upon Nebuchadnezzar's mind. Seeing this, the wise men who had been unable to tell his dream, proposed that he make an image similar to the one seen by him, and set it up where all might behold the head of gold, which was a representation of his kingdom.

This suggestion pleased the king. His pride was flattered by the thought that he could thus represent his greatness; and instead of merely reproducing the image seen in his dream, he determined to make an image that should excel the original. This image was not to deteriorate in value from the head to the feet, like the one he had been shown, but was to be composed throughout of the most precious metal. Thus the whole image would represent the greatness of Babylon; and he determined that by the splendor of this image the prophecy concerning the kingdoms which were to follow, should be effaced from his mind, and from the minds of others who had heard the dream and its interpretation.

God had spoken plainly in regard to the heavenly kingdom. "In the days of these kings," said Daniel, "shall the God of heaven set up a kingdom, which shall never be destroyed: and the kingdom shall not be left to other people, but it shall break in pieces and consume all these kingdoms, and it shall stand forever....The dream is certain, and the interpretation thereof sure."

The king had acknowledged the power of God. saying: "Of a truth it is, that your God is a God of gods,...and a revealer of secrets;" but notwithstanding this acknowledgment, the years of prosperity that followed filled his heart with pride, and he forgot God, resuming his idol-worship with increased zeal and bigotry, and cherishing the thought that the Babylonian kingdom would stand forever.

At the time when Nebuchadnezzar saw the vision of the great image, he had purposed to destroy the wise men, because he discerned their deceptions, and was convinced that they did not have the learning and power that they claimed to possess. Only by the intercession of Daniel had they been saved from a cruel and ignominious death. The king now united with these men in planning to dishonor the God of Daniel. The light that had been permitted to shine from heaven upon Nebuchadnezzar was used to serve his pride and self-exaltation. The wise men, in counsel with the king, concluded that Babylon was the kingdom which was to break in pieces all other kingdoms; and they endeavored to make an image that would represent Babylon as eternal, indestructible, all-powerful,—a kingdom that would stand forever.

From the treasures obtained in war, Nebuchadnezzar "made an image of gold, whose height was threescore cubits, and the breadth thereof six cubits: he set it up in the plain of Dura, in the province of Babylon." This image was placed in a conspicuous position, and a proclamation was issued that all should worship it.

Thus the grand lesson which God had given to the heathen through the vision of the great image, was misconstrued and misapplied. That which was designed by God to give to the world clear, distinct rays of light, Nebuchadnezzar turned from its purpose, making it minister to his pride and vanity. The prophetic illustration of God's glory was made to serve for the glorification of humanity. The symbol designed to unfold important events was used as a symbol that would hinder the spread of the knowledge that God desired the kingdoms of the world to receive. By the magnificence and beauty of his image, the king sought to make error appear more attractive, more powerful, than the truths that God had revealed.

Those who are willing to be taught, may learn a lesson from the conduct of the king of Babylon. As Satan sought to make God-given light serve his own purposes, by leading the king to work for his own glory instead of the glory of God, so the enemy works today to pervert truth in order to hinder God's purposes. Truth unmixed with error, is a power mighty to save; but if we allow the enemy to work through us; if, by means of the light given us, we seek to exalt self, even truth, perverted, may become a power for evil. —*Youth Instructor*, February 2, 1904

The Fiery Furnace

The golden image set up in the plain of Dura, an image ninety feet in height and nine in breadth, presented an imposing and majestic appearance. Nebuchadnezzar issued a proclamation, calling upon all the officers of the kingdom to assemble at the dedication of this image, and, at the sound of musical instruments, to bow down and worship it. Should any fail of doing this, they were immediately to be cast into the midst of a burning fiery furnace.

The appointed day came, and at the sound of the music the vast company that was assembled at the king's command, "fell down, and worshiped the golden image." "At that time certain Chaldeans came near,…and said to the king Nebuchadnezzar, O king, live forever….There are certain Jews whom thou hast set over the affairs of the province of Babylon, Shadrach, Meshach, and Abed-nego; these men, O king, have not regarded thee: they serve not thy gods, nor worship the golden image which thou hast set up."

Filled with rage, the king commanded that the men be brought before him. "Is it true," he inquired, "do ye not serve my gods, nor worship the golden image which I have set up?" Pointing to the angry furnace, he reminded them of the punishment that would be theirs if they refused to obey his will.

The king decided to give them a second trial. "If ye be ready," he said, "at what time ye hear the sound of the cornet, flute, harp, sackbut, psaltery, and dulcimer, and all kinds of music, ye fall down and worship the image which I have made; well; but if ye worship not, ye shall be cast the same hour into the midst of a burning fiery furnace." Then, with hand stretched upward in defiance, he asked, "And who is that God that shall deliver you out of my hands?"

In vain were the king's threats. He could not turn these noble men from their allegiance to the great Ruler of nations. From the history of their fathers, they had learned that disobedience to God results in dishonor, disaster, and death; that the fear of the Lord is not only the beginning of wisdom, but the foundation of all true prosperity. They knew that they owed to God every faculty they possessed; and while their hearts were full of generous sympathy toward all men, they had a lofty aspiration to prove themselves loyal to God.

When the king was troubled in regard to his dream, these men, with Daniel, had fasted and prayed, that they might understand the dream. The Lord had heard their cries, and he had given to Daniel wisdom to interpret the dream to the king. Thus their own lives and the lives of the astrologers and soothsayers had been saved. Now the very men who had escaped death through the mercy of God to his servants, had been the prime movers in securing the decree in regard to the worship of the golden image. But the three Hebrews made no mention of these things; they knew that a controversy with the king would only increase his fury.

Standing before the angry monarch, with the image in sight, and the sound of the entrancing music in their ears, these young men thought of the promise made to the prophet Isaiah more than one hundred years before: "Fear not: for I have redeemed thee, I have called thee by thy name; thou art mine. When thou passest through the waters, I will be with thee; when thou walkest through the fire, thou shalt not be burned, neither shall the flame kindle upon thee."

The answer of Shadrach, Meshach, and Abed-nego was respectful, but decided. Looking with calmness upon the fiery furnace and the idolatrous throng, they said: "O Nebuchadnezzar, we are not careful to answer thee in this matter. If it be so [if this be your decision], our God whom we serve will deliver us out of thine hand, O king." These Hebrew youth had unquestioning faith in God, and they were determined to honor him at any cost. Their faith strengthened with the declaration that God would be glorified by delivering them, and with a triumphant ring of trust in their voices, they added: "But if not, be it known unto thee, O king, that we will not serve thy gods, nor worship the golden image which thou hast set up." —*Youth Instructor*, March 8, 1904

The proud monarch was surrounded by his great men, the officers of the government, and the army that had conquered nations; and all united in applauding him as having the wisdom and power of the gods. In the midst of this imposing display stood the three youthful Hebrews, steadily persisting in their refusal to obey the king's decree. They had been obedient to the laws of Babylon, so far as these did not conflict with the claims of God; but they would not be swayed a hair's breadth from the duty they owed to their Creator.

The king's wrath knew no bounds. In the very height of his power and glory, to be thus defied by the representatives of a despised and captive race was an insult which his proud spirit could not endure. He commanded that the furnace be heated seven times hotter than was its wont. And without delay the Hebrew exiles were cast in. So furious were the flames, that the men who cast the Hebrews in were burned to death.

Suddenly the countenance of the king paled with terror. He looked intently upon the glowing flames, and, turning to his lords, in tones of alarm inquired, "Did we not cast three men bound into the midst of the fire?" The answer was, "True, O king." His voice trembling with excitement, the monarch exclaimed, "Lo, I see four men loose, walking in the midst of the fire, and they have no hurt; and the form of the fourth is like the Son of God"!

When Christ manifests himself to the children of men, an unseen Power speaks to their souls. They realize that they are in the presence of the Infinite One. Before his majesty, kings and nobles tremble, and acknowledge the living God as above every earthly power. The Hebrew captives had told Nebuchadnezzar of Christ, the Redeemer that was to come, and from the description thus given, the king recognized the form of the fourth in the fiery furnace as the Son of God.

His own greatness and dignity forgotten, Nebuchadnezzar descended from his throne, and hastened to the furnace. With remorse and shame he cried, "Ye servants of the most high God, come forth." And they obeyed, before that vast multitude showing themselves unhurt, not even the smell of fire being upon their garments. True to duty, they had been proof against the flames. Only their fetters had been burned.

"Then Nebuchadnezzar spake, and said, Blessed be the God of Shadrach, Meshach, and Abed-nego, who hath sent his angel, and delivered his servants that trusted in him, and have changed the king's word, and yielded their bodies, that they might not serve nor worship any god, except their own God."

A change passed over the multitude. The great golden image, set up with such display, was forgotten. Men feared and trembled before the living God. The king published a decree that any one speaking against the God of the Hebrews should be put to death; "because there is no other god that can deliver after this sort."

True Christian principle does not stop to weigh consequences. It does not ask, What will people think of me if I do this? or, How will it affect my worldly prospects if I do that? With singleness of purpose, the children of God desire to know what he would have them do, that their works may glorify him. The Lord has made ample provision that the hearts and lives of his followers shall be controlled by divine grace, that they may be as burning and shining lights in the world.

These faithful Hebrews possessed great natural ability; they had enjoyed the highest intellectual culture, and now occupied positions of honor; but they did not forget God. Their powers were yielded to the sanctifying influence of his grace. By their steadfast integrity, they showed forth the praises of him who had called them out of darkness into his marvelous light. In their wonderful deliverance were displayed, before that vast assembly, the power and majesty of God. Jesus stood by their side in the fiery furnace, and the glory of his presence convinced the proud king of Babylon that it could be no other than the Son of God. The light of heaven had been shining forth from Daniel and his companions, until all their associates understood the faith that ennobled their lives and beautified their characters. By the deliverance of his faithful servants, the Lord declares that he will take his stand with the oppressed, and overthrow all earthly powers that would trample upon the authority of the God of heaven.

What a lesson is here given to the faint-hearted, the vacillating, the cowardly in the cause of God! What encouragement to those who will not be turned aside from duty by threats or peril! These faithful, steadfast characters exemplify sanctification, while they have no thought of claiming the high honor. The amount of good which may be accomplished by comparatively obscure but devoted Christians, can not be estimated until the life-records shall be made known, when the judgment shall sit, and the books shall be opened.

Christ identifies his interest with this class; he is not ashamed to call them brethren. There should be hundreds, where there is now one among us, so closely allied to God, their lives so closely conformed to his will, that they would be bright and shining lights, sanctified wholly, in body, soul, and spirit.

The conflict still goes on between the children of light and the children of darkness. Those who name the name of Christ should shake off the lethargy that enfeebles their efforts, and should fulfil the momentous responsibilities that devolve upon them. All who do this may expect the power of God to be revealed in them. The Son of God, the world's Redeemer, will be represented in their words and in their works, and God's name will be glorified. —*Youth Instructor*, April 26, 1904

The Sabbath Test

Daniel and his companions had a conscience void of offense toward God. But this was not preserved without a struggle. What a test was brought on the three associates of Daniel, when they were required to worship the great image set up by King Nebuchadnezzar in the plain of Dura!

The three Hebrews were called upon to confess Christ in the face of the burning fiery furnace. It cost them something to do this, for their lives were at stake. These youth, imbued with the Holy Spirit, declared to the whole kingdom of Babylon their faith,—that He whom they worshiped was the only true and living God. The demonstration of their faith on the plain of Dura was a most eloquent presentation of their principles.

The lessons we may learn from the loyalty of the Hebrew captives toward God and his law, have a direct and vital bearing upon our experience in these last days. We have a confession to make different from that which we have made; and we shall have to make it under trying circumstances. In order to impress idolaters with the power and greatness of the living God, we, as his servants, must reveal our own reverence for God. We must make it manifest that he is the only object of our adoration and worship, and that no consideration, not even the preservation of life, can induce us to make the least concession to idolatry.

The vainglory and oppression seen in the course pursued by the heathen king, Nebuchadnezzar, is being and will continue to be manifested in our day. History will repeat itself. In this age the test will be on the point of Sabbath observance. The heavenly universe behold men trampling upon the law of Jehovah, making the memorial of God, the sign between him and his commandment-keeping people, a thing of naught, something to be despised, while a rival sabbath is exalted as was the great golden image in the plain of Dura. Men claiming to be Christians will call upon the world to observe this spurious sabbath that they have made. All who refuse will be placed under oppressive laws. This is the mystery of iniquity, the devising of satanic agencies, carried into effect by the man of sin.

The people of God will enter into no controversy with the world over this matter. They will simply take God's Word for their guide, and maintain their allegiance to him whose commandments they keep. They will obey the words of Jehovah: "Verily my Sabbaths ye shall keep: for it is a sign between me and you throughout your generations; that ye may know that I am the Lord that doth sanctify you. Ye shall keep the Sabbath there-fore…for a perpetual covenant."

When the Sabbath becomes the special point of controversy throughout Christendom, the persistent refusal of a small minority to yield to the popular demand will make them objects of universal execration. It will be urged that the few who stand in opposition to an institution of the church and a law of the state, ought not to be tolerated; that it is better for them to suffer than for whole nations to be thrown into confusion and lawlessness. This argument will appear conclusive; and against those who hallow the Sabbath of the fourth commandment will finally be issued a decree, denounc-ing them as deserving of the severest punishment, and giving the people liberty, after a certain time, to put them to death. Romanism in the Old World, and apostate Protestantism in the New, will pursue a similar course toward those who honor all the divine precepts.

The season of distress and anguish before us will require a faith that can endure weariness, delay, and hunger,—a faith that will not faint, though severely tried. Those who now exercise but little faith are in the greatest danger of falling under the power of satanic delusions and the decree to compel conscience. And even if they endure the test, they will be plunged into deeper distress and anguish in the time of trouble, because they have not made it a habit to trust in God. The lessons of faith which they have neglected, they will be forced to learn under a terrible pressure of discouragement.

We should now acquaint ourselves with God by proving his promises. Angels record every prayer that is earnest and sincere. We should rather dispense with selfish gratifications than neglect communion with God. The deepest poverty, the greatest self-denial, with his approval, is better than riches, honors, ease, and friendship without it. We must take time to pray. The youth would not be seduced into sin if they would refuse to enter any path save that upon which they could ask God's blessing.

My dear young friends, if you are called to go through a fiery furnace for Christ's sake, Jesus will be by your side. To you he declares: "When thou passest through the waters, I will be with thee; and through the rivers, they shall not overflow thee; when thou walkest through the fire, thou shalt not be burned; neither shall the flame kindle upon thee."

The threats of men sink into insignificance beside the word of the living God. Be loyal and true, and the God who walked with the three Hebrew children in the fiery furnace, who manifested himself to John on the lonely island, will be with you. His abiding presence will comfort and sustain you, and you will realize the fulfilment of the promise, "If a man love me, he will keep my words: and my Father will love him, and we will come unto him, and make our abode with him. —*Youth Instructor*, July 12, 1904

A Season of Splendor

Nebuchadnezzar was the greatest ruler of the age in which he lived. Ezekiel spoke of him as "a king of kings" and prophesied that God would allow him to complete the destruction of Jerusalem, and that because the inhabitants of "the renowned city" of Tyre would say against Jerusalem "Aha, she is broken that was the gates of the people: she is turned unto me: I shall be replenished, now she is laid waste," God would "bring upon Tyrus Nebuchadnezzar king of Babylon," "the terrible of the nations" who would make this place "in the midst of the seas" " a desolate city" that should be "built no more." The prophet further declared: "Nebuchadnezzar king of Babylon caused his army to serve a great service against Tyrus:...yet he had no wages, nor his army;...therefore thus saith the Lord God:...I have given him the land of Egypt for his labor wherewith he served against it, because they wrought for me."

The capital of Nebuchadnezzar's world-empire is spoken of by Isaiah as "Babylon, the glory of kingdoms, the beauty of the Chaldee's excellency," "the golden city;" "the lady of the kingdoms" "that dwellest upon many waters, abundant in treasures;" and by Jeremiah as "the praise of the whole earth." Jeremiah also speaks of "the broad walls of Babylon...and her high gates;" Isaiah, of her "gates of brass."

Habakkuk describes the Babylonians as "that bitter and hasty nation,...terrible and dreadful....Their horses also are swifter than leopards, and are more fierce than the evening wolves." Jeremiah writes in regard to "the mighty men of Babylon."

Nebuchadnezzar was an instrument of God's judgments. "Thus saith the Lord:...I have made the earth, the man and the beast that are upon the ground, by my great power and by my outstretched arm, and have given it unto whom it seemed meet unto me. And now have I given all these lands into the hand of Nebuchadnezzar the king of Babylon, my servant; and the beasts of the field have I given him also to serve him. And it shall come to pass, that the nation and kingdom which will not serve the same Nebuchadnezzar the king of Babylon, and that will not put their neck under the yoke of the king of Babylon, that nation will I punish, saith the Lord, with the sword, and with the famine, and with the pestilence, until I have consumed them by his hand. Therefore harken not ye to your prophets, nor to your diviners, nor to your dreamers, nor to your enchanters, nor to your sorcerers, which speak unto you, saying, Ye shall not serve the king of Babylon: for they prophesy a lie unto you, to remove you far from your land; and that I should drive you out, and ye should perish. But the nations that bring their neck under the yoke of the king of Babylon, and serve him, those will I let remain still in their own land, saith the Lord; and they shall till it, and dwell therein."

The vision of the great image, in which Babylon was repre-sented as the head of gold, was given Nebuchadnezzar in order that he might have a clear understanding in regard to the end of all things earthly, and also in regard to the setting up of God's everlasting kingdom. Although in the interpretation he was declared to be "a king of kings," this was because "the God of heaven" had given him "a kingdom, power, and strength, and glory." His kingdom was universal, extending "wheresoever the children of men dwell," yet it was to be followed by three other universal kingdoms, after which "the God of heaven" would "set up a kingdom," which should "never be destroyed."

In the providence of God, Nebuchadnezzar was given ample opportunity to ascribe to the Lord the glory for the splendor of his reign. And for a time after the vision of the great image, he acknowledged God as supreme. Falling back into idolatrous habits, he was again, by the miraculous deliverance of the three Hebrews from the fiery furnace, led to acknowledge that God's "kingdom is an everlasting kingdom, and his dominion is from generation to generation." But once more the king perverted the warnings God had given him, and turned aside from the path of humility to follow the imaginations of his naturally proud heart. Thinking that his kingdom should be more extensive and powerful than any that would follow, he made great additions to the city of Babylon, and gave himself up to a life of pleasure and self-glorification. Of this time he himself says: "I Nebuchadnezzar was at rest in mine house, and flourishing in my palace.—*Youth Instructor*, October 11, 1904

Nebuchadnezzar's Second Dream

Because Nebuchadnezzar did not continue to walk in the light he had received from heaven, he lost the holy impressions that had been made upon his mind. But God, in his mercy, gave the king another dream, to save him, if possible, from appropriating to himself the glory that belonged to the Supreme Ruler.

The dream given at this time to the king of Babylon was a very striking one. In a vision of the night he saw a great tree growing in the midst of the earth, towering to the heavens, and its branches stretching to the ends of the earth. "The leaves thereof were fair, and the fruit thereof much, and in it was meat for all: the beasts of the field had shadow under it, and the fowls of the heaven dwelt in the boughs thereof, and all flesh was fed of it."

As the king gazed upon that lofty tree, he beheld "a Watcher," even "an Holy One,"—a divine Messenger, similar in appearance to the One who walked with the Hebrews in the fiery furnace. This heavenly Being approached the tree, and in a loud voice cried:—

"Hew down the tree, and cut off his branches, shake off his leaves, and scatter his fruit; let the beasts get away from under it, and the fowls from his branches: nevertheless, leave the stump of his roots in the earth, even with a band of iron and brass, in the tender grass of the field; and let it be wet with the dew of heaven, and let his portion be with the beasts in the grass of the earth: let his heart be changed from man's, and let a beast's heart be given unto him; and let seven times pass over him. This matter is by the decree of the watchers, and the demand by the word of the holy ones: to the intent that the living may know that the Most High ruleth in the kingdom of men, and giveth it to whomsoever he will, and setteth up over it the basest of men."

The king was greatly troubled by this dream. It was evidently a prediction of adversity. He repeated it to the magicians, the Chaldeans, and the soothsayers; but although the dream was very explicit, none of the wise men would attempt to interpret it. Those who neither loved nor feared God could not understand the mysteries of the kingdom of heaven. They could not approach unto the throne of him who dwelleth in light unapproachable. To them the things of God must remain mysteries.

In this idolatrous nation testimony was again borne to the fact that only the servants of God can understand the mysteries of God. In the early days of the king's acquaintance with Daniel, he had found that this man was the only one who could relieve him from perplexity; and now, in this later period of his reign, the king remembers his faithful servant of old,—a servant esteemed because of his unswerving integrity and constant faithfulness. Nebuchadnezzar knew that Daniel's wisdom was unexcelled, and that neither he nor his three fellow captives ever compromised principle in order to secure position in the court, or even to preserve life itself. The skill of his wise men proving ineffectual, the king sent for Daniel to interpret the dream. —*Youth Instructor*, November 1, 1904

Losing Focus

From the record of Nebuchadnezzar's experience we may learn how the Lord regards the spirit of self-exaltation. Had the Babylonian king heeded God's warnings in regard to self-exaltation, the humiliation with which he was threatened might have been averted; but he went on with proud superiority, using the gifts of God as his own to exalt self, until he felt the humbling hand of the Almighty. Not until he had passed through seven years of shame and suffering, did the king learn that God is able to abase those who walk in pride and self-exaltation. Nebuchadnezzar's experience is a warning to all.

The Creator has given abundant evidence that his power is unlimited, that he can establish kingdoms, and overturn kingdoms. He upholds the world by the word of his power. He made the night, marshaling the shining stars in the firmament. He calls them all by name. The heavens declare the glory of God, and the firmament showeth his handiwork, showing man that this little world is but a jot in God's creation. Should every member of the human family refuse to acknowledge him, saying, There is no God, he would not want for subjects to proclaim his power.

The inhabitants of the unfallen worlds look with pity and reproach on man's pride and self-importance. The wealthy and the honored of the world are not the only ones who glorify self. Many who profess to revere God, talk of their wisdom and their might. They act as if God is under obligations to them, as if he can not carry on his work without their aid. Let such gaze into the starry heavens, and with admiration and awe study the marvelous works of God. Let them think of the wisdom he displays in maintaining perfect order in the vast universe, and of the little reason that man has to boast of his attainments.

All that man has—life, the means of existence, happiness, and other blessings unnumbered that come to him day by day—is from the Father above. Man is a debtor for all he proudly claims as his own. God gives his precious gifts, that they may be used in his service. Every particle of the glory of man's success belongs to God. It is his manifold wisdom that is displayed in the works of men, and to him belongs the praise.

Every moment the Lord's grace is exercised in behalf of human agencies. Unless the Lord keeps the heart, we are overcome by the enemy. It is Satan who perverts man's powers, and fills the heart with thoughts of self-exaltation. To fear the Lord in holiness, to walk before him in contrition and humility, is the only way to true exaltation, for nations and for individuals; while to walk boastingly and proudly, in presumptuousness and transgression, ends in speedy humiliation, defeat, and ruin.

Men may forget, men may deny their wrong course of action, but a record of it is kept in the book of remembrance, and in the great day of judgment, unless men repent and walk humbly before God, they will meet this dread record just as it stands. If they repent, and keep the fear of the Lord before them, their sins will be blotted out.

God is infinitely gracious. He waits for us to return to him by heart-humiliation, confession, and repentance. He will have mercy on all, and will save all who cherish contrition of soul. The renunciation of self-confidence prepares the way for true faith in God. The moment human beings renounce their selfishness, covetousness, and idolatry, that moment God becomes their all-sufficient Helper. In the infinite fulness of his grace he imparts, for time and for eternity, whatever is needed for the souls and bodies of those who believe.

O that those upon whom light has been shining in rich abundance, might become humble, faithful men and women! O that they would, like the king of Babylon, raise their voices in recognition of God, revealing that they have come to their senses, and that their heart of stone has been changed to a heart of flesh!

Then they might form the cabinet of God, being made, in truth, guardians of sacred trusts. —*Youth Instructor*, April 4, 1905

Nebuchadnezzar's Metamorphosis

For many months after Nebuchadnezzar's dream in regard to his humiliation, his position was unaltered. The judgment of God lingered. The king lost confidence in the dream, and regarded it as a delusion. More proud and haughty than ever, he jested at his former fears.

About a year after the king had received the divine warning, he was walking in his palace, and thinking with pride of his power as the ruler of the greatest universal kingdom, when he exclaimed, "Is not this great Babylon, that I have built for the house of the kingdom by the might of my power, and for the honor of my majesty?"

The proud boast had scarcely left his lips when a voice from heaven announced to him that God's appointed time of judgment had come. Upon his ears fell the mandate of the Almighty: "O king Nebuchadnezzar, to thee it is spoken; The kingdom is departed from thee. And they shall drive thee from men, and thy dwelling shall be with the beasts of the field: they shall make thee to eat grass as oxen, and seven times shall pass over thee, until thou know that the Most High ruleth in the kingdom of men, and giveth it to whomsoever he will."

In a moment Nebuchadnezzar's reason was taken away, and he was placed on a level with the beasts of the field. "He was driven from men, and did eat grass as oxen, and his body was wet with the dew of heaven, till his hairs were grown like eagles' feathers, and his nails like birds' claws."

As the beasts have no knowledge of God, and therefore do not acknowledge his sovereignty, so Nebuchadnezzar had been unmindful of God and his mercies. Prosperity and popularity had led him to feel independent of God, and to use for his own glory the talent of reason that God had entrusted to him. Messages of warning were sent to him, but he heeded them not. The heavenly Watcher took cognizance of the king's spirit and actions, and in a moment stripped the proud boaster of all that his Creator had given him.

Nebuchadnezzar did not profit by the warnings he received. Only through severest discipline did he learn the lesson that the Lord, and not man, is ruler, and that God's kingdom endures forever. Only after passing through long years of humiliation did the king of Babylon learn that it was not his scepter, but the scepter of him whose kingdom is everlasting, that held supreme sway over the affairs of the nations.

Man may lift himself up in pride and boast of his power, but in an instant God can bring him to nothingness. It is Satan's work to lead men to glorify themselves with their entrusted talents. Every man through whom God works will have to learn that the living, ever-present, ever-acting God is supreme, and has lent him talents to use,—an intellect to originate; a heart to be the seat of his throne; affections to flow out in blessing to all with whom he shall come in contact; a conscience through which the Holy Spirit can convict him of sin, of righteousness, and of judgment.

God is infinitely holy, and he hates every species of iniquity. He is great in power, and he will punish the mightiest with the most depraved. He first gives to transgressors oft-repeated warnings. If the heart is hardened, if it refuses to heed the warnings given, and to accept the means of salvation, God will make men feel that as he has exalted and favored them, so he has to do with their casting down. When God has forsaken those whom he has highly favored, no earthly power can avail. God is long-suffering, not willing that any should perish; but his forbearance has a limit, and when the boundary is passed, there is no second probation. His wrath will go forth, and he will destroy without remedy. —*Youth Instructor*, March 28, 1905

Restoration of Nebuchadnezzar

For seven years Nebuchadnezzar, in his degradation, was an astonishment to all his subjects. For seven years he was humbled before the world, as a punishment for ascribing to himself the glory that belonged to God. At the end of this time his reason was restored to him. Through his terrible humiliation he was brought to see his own weakness, and to acknowledge the supremacy of God.

In the book of Daniel is given the king's public confession of his restoration. We read: "At the end of the days I Nebuchadnezzar lifted up mine eyes unto heaven, and mine understanding returned unto me, and I blessed the Most High, and I praised and honored him that liveth forever, whose dominion is an everlasting dominion, and his kingdom is from generation to generation: and all the inhabitants of the earth are reputed as nothing: and he doeth according to his will in the army of heaven, and among the inhabitants of the earth: and none can stay his hand, or say to him,. What doest thou? At the same time my reason returned unto me; and for the glory of my kingdom, mine honor and brightness returned unto me; and my counselors and my lords sought unto me; and I was established in my kingdom, and excellent majesty was added unto me."

The chastening that came upon the king of Babylon wrought reformation in his heart, and transformed him in character. He now understands God's purpose in humiliating him. In this chastisement he recognizes the divine hand. Before his humiliation he was tyrannical in his dealings with others, but now the fierce, over-bearing monarch is changed into a wise and compassionate ruler. Before his humiliation he defied and blasphemed the God of heaven, but now he humbly acknowledges the power of the Most High, and earnestly seeks to promote the happiness of his subjects.

At last, under the rebuke of God, the king had learned the lesson which all kings and rulers need to learn,—that true greatness consists in goodness. He acknowledged Jehovah as the living God, saying: Come, all ye that fear God, and I will make known to you what he hath done for my soul. It is now my wish that all the people of my realm shall learn what I have learned, that the God whom they should worship is not a golden image, but he who made the heavens and the earth. "I Nebuchadnezzar praise and extol, and honor the King of heaven, all whose works are truth, and his ways judgment: and those that walk in pride he is able to abase."

Thus the king upon the Babylonian throne became a witness for God, giving his testimony, warm and eloquent, from a grateful heart that was partaking of the mercy and grace, the righteousness and peace, of the divine nature. God's design that the greatest kingdom of the world should show forth his praise, was now fulfilled.

The public proclamation in which Nebuchadnezzar acknowledged his guilt and the great mercy of God in his restoration, is the last act of his life as recorded in Sacred History. —*Youth Instructor*, December 13, 1904

69

The Secret Watcher

"I saw in the visions of my head upon my bed," writes Daniel, "and, behold, a watcher and an holy one came down from heaven; he cried aloud, and said thus, Hew down the tree, and cut off his branches, shake off his leaves, and scatter his fruit: let the beasts get away from under it, and the fowls from his branches: nevertheless leave the stump of his roots in the earth, even with a band of iron and brass, in the tender grass of the field; and let it be wet with the dew of heaven, and let his portion be with the beasts in the grass of the earth: let his heart be changed from man's, and let a beast's heart be given unto him; and let seven times pass over him. This matter is by the decree of the watchers, and the demand by the word of the holy ones: to the intent that the living may know that the Most High ruleth in the kingdom of men, and giveth it to whomsoever he will."

Here we are shown that God holds even heathen kings subject to his will. He takes idolaters, and deals with them according to their evil ways and doings.

The same Watcher who came to Daniel was an uninvited guest at Belshazzar's sacrilegious feast. This monarch had everything to flatter his pride and indulge his passions. He was a great king, presiding over what was then the greatest kingdom on earth. His provinces were cultivated by captives, and his capital was enriched by the spoil of nations. He held the life and property of his subjects in his hand. To those who ministered to his pride and vanity, he was indulgent; they were his chosen favorites; but if at any moment they crossed his will, he was at once a cruel tyrant. His anger blazed forth against them without restraint.

Admitted to a share in kingly authority at fifteen years of age, Belshazzar gloried in his power, and lifted up his heart against the God of heaven. He despised the One who is above all rulers, the General of all the armies of heaven. "Belshazzar the king made a great feast to a thousand of his lords, and drank wine before the thousand." On this occasion there was music and dancing and wine-drinking. The profane orgies of royal mirth were attended by men of genius and education. Decorated women with their enchantments, were among the revelers.

Exalted by wine and blinded by delusion, the king himself took the lead in the riotous blasphemy. Reason no longer controlled him; his lower impulses and passions were in the ascendency. His kingdom was strong and apparently invincible, and he would show that he thought nothing too sacred for his hands to handle and profane. To show his contempt for sacred things, he desecrated the holy vessels taken from the temple of the Lord at its destruction.

A Watcher, who was unrecognized, but whose presence was a power of condemnation, looked on this scene of profanation. Soon the unseen and uninvited Guest made his presence felt. At the moment when the sacrilegious revelry was at its height, a bloodless hand came forth, and wrote words of doom on the wall of the banqueting hall. Burning words followed the movements of the hand. "Mene, Mene, Tekel, Upharsin," was written in letters of flame. Few were the characters traced by that hand on the wall facing the king, but they showed that the power of God was there.

Belshazzar was afraid. His conscience was awakened. The fear and suspicion that always follow the course of the guilty seized him. When God makes men fear, they can not hide the intensity of their terror. Alarm seized the great men of the kingdom. Their blasphemous disrespect of sacred things was changed in a moment. A frantic terror overcame all self-control.

Belshazzar had been given many opportunities for knowing and doing the will of God. He had seen his grandfather Nebuchadnezzar banished from the society of men. He had seen the intellect in which the proud monarch gloried taken away by the One who gave it. He had seen the king driven from his kingdom, and made the companion of the beasts of the field. But Belshazzar's love of amusement and self-glorification effaced the lessons he should never have forgotten; and he committed sins similar to those that brought signal judgments on Nebuchadnezzar. He wasted the opportunities graciously granted him, neglecting to use the opportunities within his reach for becoming acquainted with truth. "What must I do to be saved?" was a question that the great but foolish king passed by indifferently.

This is the danger of heedless, reckless youth today. The hand of God will awaken the sinner as it did Belshazzar, but with many it will be too late to repent.

The ruler of Babylon had riches and honor, and in his haughty self-indulgence he had lifted himself up against the God of heaven and earth. He had trusted in his own arm, not supposing that any would dare to say, "Why doest thou this?" But as the mysterious hand traced letters on the wall of his palace, Belshazzar was awed and silenced. In a moment he was completely shorn of his strength, and humbled as a child. He realized that he was at the mercy of One greater than himself. He had been making sport of sacred things. Now his conscience was awakened. He realized that he had had the privilege of knowing and doing the will of God. The history of his grandfather stood out as vividly before him as the writing on the wall.

In vain the king tried to read the burning letters. He had found a power too strong for him. He could not read the writing. "The king cried aloud to bring in the astrologers, the Chaldeans, and the soothsayers. And the king spake, and said to the wise men of Babylon, Whosoever shall read this writing, and show me the interpretation thereof, shall be clothed with scarlet, and have a chain of gold about his neck, and shall be the third ruler in the kingdom. Then came in all the king's wise men: but they could not read the writing, nor make known to the king the interpretation thereof." In vain the king offered honor and promotion. Heavenly wisdom can not be bought and sold. "Then was king Belshazzar greatly troubled, and his countenance was changed in him, and his lords were astonished." —*Youth Instructor*, May 19, 1898

There was in the palace a woman who was wiser than them all,—the queen of Belshazzar's grandfather. In this emergency she addressed the king in language that sent a ray of light into the darkness. "O king, live forever," she said; "let not thy thoughts trouble thee, nor let thy countenance be changed: there is a man in thy kingdom, in whom is the spirit of the holy gods; and in the days of thy father light and understanding and wisdom, like the wisdom of the gods, was found in him; whom the king Nebuchadnezzar thy father, the king, I say, thy father, made master of the magicians, astrologers, Chaldeans, and soothsayers:…now let Daniel be called, and he will show the interpretation."

"Then was Daniel brought in before the king." Making an effort to brace himself, and to show his authority, Belshazzar said: "Art thou that Daniel, which art of the children of the captivity of Judah, whom the king my father brought out of Jewry? I have even heard of thee, that the spirit of the gods is in thee, and that light and understanding and excellent wisdom is found in thee….Now if thou canst read the writing, and make known to me the interpretation thereof, thou shalt be clothed with scarlet, and have a chain of gold about thy neck, and shalt be the third ruler in the kingdom."

Daniel was not awed by the king's appearance, nor confused or intimidated by his words. "Let thy gifts be to thyself," he answered, "and give thy rewards to another; yet I will read the writing unto the king, and make known to him the interpretation. O thou king, the most high God gave Nebuchadnezzar thy father a kingdom, and majesty, and glory, and honor….But when his heart was lifted up, and his mind hardened in pride, he was deposed from his kingly throne, and they took his glory from him….And thou his son, O Belshazzar, hast not humbled thine heart, though thou knewest all this; but hast lifted up thyself against the Lord of heaven; and they have brought the vessels of his house before thee, and thou, and thy lords, thy wives, and thy concubines, have drunk in them; and thou hast praised the gods of silver, and gold, of brass, iron, wood, and stone, which see not, nor hear, nor know: and the God in whose hand thy breath is, and whose are all thy ways, hast thou not glorified."

"This is the writing that was written, Mene, Mene, Tekel, Upharsin. This is the interpretation of the thing: Mene; God hath numbered thy kingdom, and finished it. Tekel; Thou art weighed in the balances, and art found wanting. Peres; Thy kingdom is divided, and given to the Medes and Persians."

Daniel did not swerve from his duty. He held the king's sin before him, showing him the lessons he might have learned, but did not. Belshazzar had not heeded the events so significant to him. He had not read his grandfather's history correctly. The responsibility of knowing truth had been laid upon him, but the practical lessons he might have learned and acted upon had not been taken to heart; and his course of action brought the sure result.

This was the last feast of boasting held by the Chaldean king; for he who bears long with man's perversity had passed the irrevocable sentence. Belshazzar had greatly dishonored the One who had exalted him as king, and his probation was taken from him. While the king and his nobles were at the height of their revelry, the Persians turned the Euphrates out of its channel, and marched into the unguarded city. As Belshazzar and his lords were drinking from the sacred vessels of Jehovah, and praising their gods of silver and gold, Cyrus and his soldiers stood under the walls of the palace. "In that night," the record says, "was Belshazzar the king of the Chaldeans slain. And Darius the Median took the kingdom."

Could the curtain be rolled back before the youth who have never given their hearts to God, with others who are Christians in name, but who are unrenewed in heart and unsanctified in temper, they would see that God's eye is ever upon them, and they would feel as disturbed as did the king of Babylon. They would realize that in every place, at every hour in the day, there is a holy Watcher, who balances every account, whose eye takes in the whole situation, whether it is one of fidelity, or one of disloyalty and deception.

We are never alone. We have a Companion, whether we choose him or not. Remember, young men and young women, that wherever you are, whatever you are doing, God is there. To your every word and action you have a witness,—the holy, sin-hating God. Nothing that is said or done or thought can escape his infinite eye. Your words may not be heard by human ears, but they are heard by the Ruler of the universe. He reads the inward anger of the soul when the will is crossed. He hears the expression of profanity. In the deepest darkness and solitude he is there. No one can deceive God; none can escape from their accountability to him.

"O Lord, thou hast searched me, and known me," writes the psalmist. "Thou knowest my downsitting and mine uprising, thou understandest my thought afar off. Thou compassest my path and my lying down, and art acquainted with all my ways. For there is not a word in my tongue, but, lo, O Lord, thou knowest it altogether. Thou hast beset me behind and before, and laid thine hand upon me. Such knowledge is too wonderful for me; it is high; I can not attain unto it. Whither shall I go from thy Spirit? or whither shall I flee from thy presence? If I ascend up into heaven, thou art there: If I make my bed in hell, behold, thou art there. If I take the wings of the morning, and dwell in the uttermost parts of the sea; even there shall thy hand lead me, and thy right hand shall hold me. If I say, Surely the darkness shall cover me; even the night shall be light about me. Yea, the darkness hideth not from thee; but the night shineth as the day: the darkness and the light are both alike to thee."

Day by day the record of your words, your actions, and your influence, is being made in the books of heaven. This you must meet. "I saw the dead, small and great, stand before God; and the books were opened: and another book was opened, which is the book of life: and the dead were judged out of those things which were written in the books, according to their works....And whosoever was not found written in the book of life was cast into the lake of fire."

I send you the note of warning to take heed. You are appointed to be "laborers together with God." This responsibility you may ignore; but your action in so doing will bring its sure result. God has given to each of you your work. He has given you faculties, means, light, and knowledge, and he holds you accountable for the way in which you use these powers. "We ought to give the more earnest heed to the things which we have heard, lest at any time we should let them slip. For if the word spoken by angels was steadfast, and every transgression and disobedience received a just recompense of reward; how shall we escape, if we neglect so great salvation; which at the first began to be spoken by the Lord, and was confirmed unto us by them that heard him?"
—*Youth Instructor*, May 26, 1898

In the Lion's Den

Under the reign of Darius, Daniel was exalted to a position of great honor, because the king saw in him an "excellent spirit." But when the leading men of the kingdom saw Daniel thus favored, they became jealous of him, and soon envied and hated him. His course of unbending integrity was in marked contrast to their own lives. The more upright and righteous he was, the more they hated him. Long they sought to find something whereby he might be condemned. It angered them to think that they could lay nothing to his charge. But he was prime minister of the kingdom, and they knew they would have to prove any charge they brought against him.

Daniel's position was not an enviable one. He stood at the head of a dishonest, prevaricating, godless cabinet, whose members watched him with keen, jealous eyes, to find some flaw in his conduct. They kept spies on his track, to see if they could not in this way find something against him. Satan suggested to these men a plan whereby they might get rid of Daniel. Use his religion as a means of condemning him, the enemy said.

Daniel was a man of prayer. Three times a day he knelt before the Lord; and Satan told his enemies that his destruction must be compassed on this ground.

A large number of the princes and nobles were in the secret, but the king was kept in ignorance of their purpose, they went to him, and asked him, in honor of his kingly dignity, to pass a decree commanding that for thirty days no one in the kingdom should ask anything of any god save Darius.

"All the presidents of the kingdom, the governors, and the princes, the counselors, and the captains have consulted together," they said, "to establish a royal statute, and to make a firm decree, that whosoever shall ask a petition of any god or man for thirty days, save of thee, O king, he shall be cast into the den of lions. Now, O king, establish the decree, and sign the writing, that it be not changed, according to the law of the Medes and Persians, which altereth not."

The king's vanity was flattered. Not for a moment did he think that Daniel, his beloved and honored servant, would in any way be affected by the law. He signed the decree, and with it in their possession, the presidents and princes went forth from his presence, evil triumph depicted on their countenances. They deemed that the man they hated was now in their power.

Daniel heard of what had been done, but he made no protest. He could see the design of his enemies. He knew that they would watch closely his going out and his coming in, but he calmly attended to his duties, and at the hour of prayer he went to his chamber, and kneeling by the open window, with his face toward Jerusalem, he prayed to his God. From his youth he had been taught that in prayer his face should be turned toward the temple, where by faith he saw the revelation of Jehovah's glory.

Daniel prayed more fervently than was his wont, that He who understands the secret working of Satan and his agents would not leave his servant, but would care for him. He prayed for strength to endure the trial.

Some may ask, Why did not Daniel lift his soul to God in secret prayer? Would not the Lord, knowing the situation, have excused his servant from kneeling openly before him? Or why did he not kneel before God in some secret place, where his enemies could not see him?

Daniel knew that the God of Israel must be honored before the Babylonian nation. He knew that neither kings nor nobles had any right to come between him and his duty to his God. He must bravely maintain his religious principles before all men; for he was God's witness. Therefore he prayed as was his wont, as if no decree had been made.

"Then these men assembled, and found Daniel praying and making supplication before his God."

Eagerly they hastened to Darius, concealing their cruel joy under a cloak of regret that they were obliged to inform against Daniel. But they declared that by Daniel's act the king's position as sovereign of the land was endangered, and his authority despised. "That Daniel, which is of the children of the captivity of Judah, regardeth not thee, O king, nor the decree that thou hast signed, but maketh his petition three times a day."

"Then the king, when he heard these words, was sore displeased with himself."

Too late he understood the snare that had been laid for the destruction of his favorite servant. Sorely troubled, he tried in every way to rescue Daniel. Till the going down of the sun he labored to deliver him. But Daniel's accusers had managed the matter so well that there was no way of escape. "Know, O king," they said, "that the law of the Medes and Persians is, That no decree nor statute which the king establisheth may be changed."

Daniel was brought before the king and his princes to answer the accusation brought against him. He had opportunity to speak for himself, and he boldly acknowledged his belief in the living God, the maker of heaven and earth. He made a noble confession of faith, relating his experience from his first connection with the kingdom.

In his perplexity and distress, Darius said to Daniel, I have done all I can to save you. I can do no more. "Thy God, whom thou servest continually, he will deliver thee," he added, as he bade him a sorrowful farewell.

Daniel was cast into the den of lions. "And a stone was brought, and laid upon the mouth of the den; and the king sealed it with his own signet, and with the signet of his lords, that the purpose might not be changed concerning Daniel." Full of satanic exultation, Daniel's enemies returned to their homes. They drank freely of wine, and congratulated themselves on their success in putting out of the way one whom they could not bribe to forsake the path of integrity.

Not so did Darius pass the night. Daniel's testimony had made a deep impression on his mind. He had some knowledge of the dealing of God with the people of Israel, and Daniel's conduct sent home to his heart the conviction, that the God of the Hebrews was the true God. He was filled with remorse for having signed the decree brought to him. His conscience was awakened, and he passed a sleepless and troubled night. The chamber of royalty was one of sorrow and prayer. All music was hushed. All amusements were laid aside. No comforters were admitted.

During that sleepless night the king thought as he had never thought before. Early the next morning, hoping and yet despairing, condemning himself, and praying to him whom he began to recognize as the true God, Darius went to the lion's den, and cried aloud: "O Daniel, servant of the living God, is thy God, whom thou servest continually, able to deliver thee from the lions?"

With intense anxiety he waited for an answer, and unspeakable thankfulness filled his heart as a voice came up from below: "O king, live forever. My God hath sent his angel, and hath shut the lions' mouths, that they have not hurt me: forasmuch as before him innocency was found in me and also before thee, O king, have I done no hurt.

"Then was the king exceeding glad for him, and commanded that they should take Daniel up out of the den. So Daniel was taken up out of the den, and no manner of hurt was found upon him, because he believed in his God." —*Youth Instructor*, November 1, 1900

"And the king commanded, and they brought those men which had accused Daniel, and they cast them into the den of lions, them, their children, and their wives; and the lions had the mastery of them, and brake all their bones in pieces or ever they came at the bottom of the den."

Once more a proclamation was issued by a heathen ruler, exalting the God of Daniel as the true God. "King Darius wrote unto all people, nations, and languages, that dwell in all the earth;

Peace be multiplied unto you. I make a decree, that in every dominion of my kingdom men tremble and fear before the God of Daniel: for He is the living God, and steadfast forever, and His kingdom that which shall not be destroyed, and His dominion shall be even unto the end. He delivereth and rescueth, and He worketh signs and wonders in heaven and in earth, who hath delivered Daniel from the power of the lions."

The wicked opposition to God's servant was now completely broken. "Daniel prospered in the reign of Darius, and in the reign of Cyrus the Persian." And through association with him, these heathen monarchs were constrained to acknowledge his God as "the living God, and steadfast forever, and His kingdom that which shall not be destroyed." —*Prophets and Kings*, 544–45

Thus the Lord cared for his faithful servant, and thus will he care for all who put their trust in him. "The angel of the Lord encampeth round about them that fear him, and delivereth them.—*Youth Instructor*, November 1, 1900

When Darius set over the provinces of his kingdom a hundred and twenty princes, and over these, three presidents, to whom the princes where to give account, we read that "Daniel was preferred above the presidents and princes, because an excellent spirit was found in him; and the king thought to set him over the whole realm." But evil angels, fearing the influence of this good man over the king and in the affairs of the kingdom, stirred up the presidents and princes to envy. These wicked men watched Daniel closely, that they might find some fault in him which they could report to the king; but they failed. "He was faithful, neither was there any error or fault found in him."

Then Satan sought to make Daniel's faithfulness to God the cause of his destruction. The presidents and princes came tumultuously together unto the king, and said, "All the presidents of the kingdom, the governors and the princes, the counselors and the captains, have consulted together to establish a royal statute, and to make a firm decree, that whosoever shall ask a petition of any God or man for thirty days, save of thee, O king, he shall be cast into the den of lions." The king's pride was flattered. He was ignorant of the mischief purposed against Daniel, and he granted their request. The decree was signed, and became one of the unalterable laws of the Medes and Persians.

These envious men did not believe that Daniel would be untrue to his God, or that he would falter in his firm adherence to principle; and they were not mistaken in their estimate of his character. Daniel knew the value of communion with God. With full knowledge of the king's decree, he still bowed in prayer three times a day, "his windows being open in his chamber toward Jerusalem." He did not seek to conceal his act, although he knew full well the consequences of his fidelity to God. He saw the dangers that beset his path; but his steps faltered not. Before those who were plotting his ruin, he would not allow even the appearance that his connection with Heaven was severed.

In all cases where the king had a right to command, Daniel would obey. He was willing to obey so far as he could do so consistently with truth and righteousness; but kings and decrees could not make him swerve from his allegiance to the King of kings. He knew that no man, not even his king, had a right to come between his conscience and his God, and interfere with the worship due to his Maker.

Daniel was true, noble, and generous. While he was anxious to be at peace with all men, he would not permit any power to turn him aside from the path of duty. He had an opportunity to testify in favor of the true God, and to present the reasons why he alone should receive worship, and the duty of rendering him praise and homage, and nobly did he improve it. Had he respected the king's decree in this instance, he would have dishonored God. He was surrounded by proud idolaters; but he was a faithful witness for the truth. His dauntless adherence to a right course of action, was as a bright light amid the moral darkness of that heathen court.

On account of his praying to God, Daniel was cast into the lion's den. Envious and wicked men thus far accomplished their purpose. But Daniel continued to pray, even among the lions. Did

God forget his faithful servant, and suffer him to be destroyed? Oh, no; Jesus, the mighty Commander of the hosts of Heaven, sent his angels to close the mouths of those hungry lions, that they should not hurt the praying man of God; and all was peace in that terrible den. The king witnessed the miraculous preservation of Daniel, and brought him out with honors; while those who had plotted his destruction were utterly destroyed, with their wives and children, in the terrible manner in which they had planned to destroy Daniel.

Through the moral courage of this one man who chose, even in the face of death, to take a right course rather than a politic one, Satan was defeated, and God honored. For the deliverance of Daniel from the power of the lions was a striking evidence that the Being whom he worshiped was the true and living God. And the king wrote unto "all people, nations, and languages, that dwell in all the earth:" "I make a decree, That in every dominion of my kingdom men tremble and fear before the God of Daniel; for he is the living God, and steadfast forever, and his kingdom that which shall not be destroyed, and his dominion shall be even unto the end."

Daniel was sorely tried; but he overcame because he was of a humble and prayerful spirit. Although he was surrounded with distrust and suspicion, and his enemies laid a snare for his life, yet he maintained a serene and cheerful trust in God, never once deviating from principle. Although Daniel was a man of like passions with ourselves, the pen of inspiration presents him as a faultless character. His life is given us as a bright example of what man may become, even in this life, if he will make God his strength, and wisely improve the privileges and opportunities within his reach. —*Signs of the Times*, November 4, 1886

Faithfulness in Duty

From the story of Daniel's deliverance we may learn that in seasons of trial and gloom God's children should be just what they were when their prospects were bright with hope and their surroundings all that they could desire. Daniel in the lions' den was the same Daniel who stood before the king as chief among the ministers of state and as a prophet of the Most High. A man whose heart is stayed upon God will be the same in the hour of his greatest trial as he is in prosperity, when the light and favor of God and of man beam upon him. Faith reaches to the unseen, and grasps eternal realities.

Heaven is very near those who suffer for righteousness' sake. Christ identifies His interests with the interests of His faithful people; He suffers in the person of His saints, and whoever touches His chosen ones touches Him. The power that is near to deliver from physical harm or distress is also near to save from the greater evil, making it possible for the servant of God to maintain his integrity under all circumstances, and to triumph through divine grace.

The experience of Daniel as a statesman in the kingdoms of Babylon and Medo-Persia reveals the truth that a businessman is not necessarily a designing, policy man, but that he may be a man instructed by God at every step. Daniel, the prime minister of the greatest of earthly kingdoms, was at the same time a prophet of God, receiving the light of heavenly inspiration. A man of like passions as ourselves, the pen of inspiration describes him as without fault. His business transactions, when subjected to the closest scrutiny of his enemies, were found to be without one flaw. He was an example of what every businessman may become when his heart is converted and consecrated, and when his motives are right in the sight of God.

Strict compliance with the requirements of Heaven brings temporal as well as spiritual blessings. Unwavering in his allegiance to God, unyielding in his mastery of self, Daniel, by his noble dignity and unswerving integrity, while yet a young man, won the "favor and tender love" of the heathen officer in whose charge he had been placed. Daniel 1:9. The same characteristics marked his afterlife. He rose speedily to the position of prime minister of the kingdom of Babylon. Through the reign of successive monarchs, the downfall of the nation, and the establishment of another world empire, such were his wisdom and statesmanship, so perfect his tact, his courtesy, his genuine goodness of heart, his fidelity to principle, that even his enemies were forced to the confession that "they could find none occasion nor fault; forasmuch as he was faithful."

Honored by men with the responsibilities of state and with the secrets of kingdoms bearing universal sway, Daniel was honored by God as His ambassador, and was given many revelations of the mysteries of ages to come. His wonderful prophecies, as recorded by him in chapters 7 to 12 of the book bearing his name, were not fully understood even by the prophet himself; but before his life labors closed, he was given the blessed assurance that "at the end of the days"—in the closing period of this world's history—he would again be permitted to stand in his lot and place. It was not given him to understand all that God had revealed of the divine purpose. "Shut up the words, and seal the book," he was directed concerning his prophetic writings; these were to be sealed "even to the time of the end." "Go thy way, Daniel," the angel once more directed the faithful messenger of Jehovah; "for the words are closed up and sealed till the time of the end....Go thou thy way till the end be: for thou shalt rest, and stand in thy lot at the end of the days." Daniel 12:4, 9, 13.

As we near the close of this world's history, the prophecies recorded by Daniel demand our special attention, as they relate to the very time in which we are living. With them should be linked the teachings of the last book of the New Testament Scriptures. Satan has led many to believe that the prophetic portions of the writings of Daniel and of John the revelator cannot be understood. But the promise is plain that special blessing will accompany the study of these prophecies. "The wise shall understand" (verse 10), was spoken of the visions of Daniel that were to be unsealed in the latter days; and of the revelation that Christ gave to His servant John for the guidance of God's people all through the centuries, the promise is, "Blessed is he that readeth, and they that hear the words of this prophecy, and keep those things which are written therein." Revelation 1:3.

From the rise and fall of nations as made plain in the books of Daniel and the Revelation, we need to learn how worthless is mere outward and worldly glory. Babylon, with all its power and magnificence, the like of which our world has never since beheld,—power and magnificence which to the people of that day seemed so stable and enduring,—how completely has it passed away! As "the flower of the grass," it has perished. James 1:10. So perished the Medo-Persian kingdom, and the kingdoms of Grecia and Rome. And so perishes all that has not God for its foundation. Only that which is bound up with His purpose, and expresses His character, can endure. His principles are the only steadfast things our world knows.

A careful study of the working out of God's purpose in the history of nations and in the revelation of things to come, will help us to estimate at their true value things seen and things unseen, and to learn what is the true aim of life. Thus, viewing the things of time in the light of eternity, we may, like Daniel and his fellows, live for that which is true and noble and enduring. And learning in this life the principles of the kingdom of our Lord and Saviour, that blessed kingdom which is to endure for ever and ever, we may be prepared at His coming to enter with Him into its possession. —*Prophets and Kings*, 545–48

Seventy Years Ended

Soon after the fall of Babylon and the beginning of the universal empire of Medo-Persia, in the first year of the reign of Darius the Mede, Daniel the prophet "understood by books the number of the years, whereof the word of the Lord came to Jeremiah the prophet, that he would accomplish seventy years in the desolations of Jerusalem."

Daniel and his companions had been taken to Babylon "in the third year of the reign of Jehoiakim king of Judah." They were members of the first company of captives whom Nebuchadnezzar brought from Jerusalem into the land of Shinar. Daniel was well acquainted with the prophecies of Jeremiah at the time they were given, and he had passed through the periods immediately succeeding the first and the second sieges of Jerusalem, when many false prophets had arisen with the claim that the captivity was to be of short duration.

"In the fourth year of Jehoiakim," very soon after Daniel was taken to Babylon, Jeremiah predicted the captivity of many of the Jews, as their punishment for not heeding the word of the Lord. The Chaldeans were to be used as the instrument by which God would chastise his disobedient people. Their punishment was to be in proportion to their intelligence and to the warnings they had despised. "This whole land shall be a desolation, and an astonishment," the prophet declared; "and these nations shall serve the king of Babylon seventy years. And it shall come to pass, when seventy years are accomplished, that I will punish the king of Babylon, and that nation, saith the Lord, for their iniquity, and the land of the Chaldeans, and will make it perpetual desolations."

In the light of these plain words foretelling the duration of the captivity, it seems strange that any one should hold that the Israelites would soon return from Babylon. And yet there were in Jerusalem and in Babylon those who persisted in encouraging the people to hope for a speedy deliverance. God dealt summarily with some of these false prophets, and thus vindicated the truthfulness of Jeremiah, his messenger.

To the end of time, men will arise to create confusion and rebellion among the people who profess to obey the law of God. But as surely as divine judgment was visited upon the false prophets in Jeremiah's day, so surely will the evil workers of today receive their full measure of retribution, for the Lord has not changed. Those who prophesy lies, encourage men to look upon sin as a light thing. When the terrible results of their evil deeds are made manifest, they seek, if possible, to make the one who has faithfully warned them responsible for their difficulties, even as the Jews charged Jeremiah with their evil fortunes.

Those who pursue a course of rebellion against the Lord can always find false prophets who will justify them in their acts, and flatter them to their destruction. Lying words often make many friends, as is illustrated in the case of these false teachers among the Israelites. These so-called prophets, in their pretended zeal for God, found many more believers and followers than the true prophet who delivered the simple message of the Lord.

In view of the work of these false prophets, Jeremiah was directed by the Lord to write letters to the captains, elders, priests, prophets, and all the people who had been taken captive to Babylon, bidding them not to be deluded into believing their deliverance nigh, but to submit quietly, pursue their vocations, and make for themselves peaceful homes among their conquerors. The Lord bade them not to allow so-called prophets or diviners to deceive them with false expectations. Through his servant Jeremiah he assured them that after seventy years' bondage they should be delivered, and should return to Jerusalem. God would listen to their prayers and show them his favor, when they would turn to him with all their hearts. "I will be found of you, saith the Lord: and I will turn away your captivity, and I will gather you from all the nations, and from all the places whither I have driven you, saith the Lord; and I will bring you again into the place whence I caused you to be carried away captive."

With what tender compassion did God inform his captive people of his plans for Israel! He knew what suffering and disaster they would have to undergo, were they led to believe, according to the prediction of the false prophets, that they should be speedily delivered and brought back to Jerusalem. He knew that this belief would make their position a very difficult one. Any effort on their part to regain freedom would awaken the vigilance and severity of the king, and their liberty would be restricted in consequence. The Lord desired them to submit quietly to their fate, and make their servitude as pleasant as possible. —*Review and Herald*, March 14, 1907

A copy of the letters sent by Jeremiah to the Hebrew captives in Babylon, and of the letters sent by the false prophets to these captives and to the authorities of Jerusalem, together with a story of the controversy between the true and false, is found in the twenty-seventh to the twenty-ninth chapters of Jeremiah.

It was immediately after this interchange of letters between Jeremiah and the elders of the Israelites in captivity, that the prophets was instructed to write in a book all that had been revealed to him regarding the restoration of Israel. This is recorded in the thirtieth and the thirty-first chapters of Jeremiah.

These, with the prophecies of the twenty-fifth chapter, are the letters and the records that Daniel the prophet, during "the first year of the reign of Darius the Mede," prayerfully studied, three-score years and more after they were written. Daniel was familiar with the circumstances connected with Jeremiah's testimonies given very soon after the beginning of the Babylonian captivity. He well knew that the promise of the return was sure; and yet, a short time before, "in the third year of the reign of King Belshazzar," the angel of the Lord had instructed him in vision,

"Unto two thousand and three hundred days; then shall the sanctuary be cleansed."

Daniel "sought for the meaning" of the vision. He could not understand the relation sustained by the seventy years' captivity to the twenty-three hundred years that were to elapse before the cleansing of God's sanctuary. Gabriel gave a partial interpretation; and when he declared that the vision "shall be for many days," Daniel fainted. "I Daniel fainted," the prophet writes, "and was sick certain days; afterward I rose up, and did the king's business; and I was astonished at the vision; but none understood it."

In his perplexity, Daniel studied anew the prophecies of Jeremiah. They were very plain,—so plain that he "understood" by these testimonies recorded in books "the number of the years, whereof the word of the Lord came to Jeremiah the prophet, that he would accomplish seventy years in the desolations of Jerusalem."

With faith founded on the sure word of prophecy, Daniel pleaded with the Lord for the speedy restoration of the captive exiles to the land of their fathers. "I set my face unto the Lord God," he declares, "to seek by prayer and supplications, with fasting, and sackcloth, and ashes: and I prayed unto the Lord my God, and made my confession." "We have sinned," he acknowledged; "neither have we obeyed the voice of the Lord our God, to walk in his laws, which he set before us by his servants the prophets."

"O Lord, according to all thy righteousness," the prophet pleaded, "let thine anger and thy fury be turned away from thy city Jerusalem, thy holy mountain: because for our sins, and for the iniquities of our fathers, Jerusalem and thy people are become a reproach to all that are about us. Now therefore, O our God, hear the prayer of thy servant, and his supplications, and cause thy face to shine upon thy sanctuary that is desolate, for the Lord's sake. O my God, incline thine ear, and hear; open thine eyes, and behold our desolations, and the city which is called by thy name: for we do not present our supplications before thee for our righteousness, but for thy great mercies. O Lord, hear; O Lord, forgive; O Lord, harken and do; defer not, for thine own sake, O my God: for thy city and thy people are called by thy name."

The prayer of Daniel was not offered in vain. Even before he had finished pleading with God, Gabriel again appeared to him, and called his attention to the vision he had seen prior to the fall of Babylon at the death of Belshazzar. The angel then outlined in detail the period of the seventy weeks, beginning at the time of "the going forth of the commandment to restore and to build Jerusalem."

Daniel's prayer in behalf of his people, as recorded in the ninth chapter, was "in the first year of Darius" the Mede. Darius was favored of heaven; for in the first year of his reign the angel Gabriel "stood up to confirm and to strengthen him." It was this king who, early in the establishment of the Medo-Persian empire, "set over the kingdom an hundred and twenty princess, which should be over the whole kingdom; and over these three presidents; of whom Daniel was first....This Daniel was preferred above the presidents and princes, because an excellent spirit was in him; and the king thought to set him over the whole realm."
—*Review and Herald*, March 21, 1907

A Sanctified Prayer

Darius reigned over Medo-Persia two years after the fall of Babylon. During this time, Daniel was cast into the lions' den and came out unharmed. This deliverance led Darius to write "unto all people, nations, and languages, that dwell in all the earth; Peace be multiplied unto you. I make a decree, That in every dominion in my kingdom men tremble and fear before the God of Daniel: for he is the living God, and steadfast forever, and his kingdom that which shall not be destroyed, and his dominion shall be even unto the end. He delivereth and rescueth, and he worketh signs and wonders in heaven and in earth, who hath delivered Daniel from the power of the lions. So this Daniel prospered in the reign of Darius, and in the reign of Cyrus the Persian."

Thus, while whose who had remained loyal to God in the midst of Babylon were seeking the Lord and studying the prophecies foretelling their deliverance, God was preparing the hearts of kings to show favor to his repentant people. —*Review and Herald*, March 21, 1907

As the time approached for the close of the seventy years' captivity, Daniel's mind became greatly exercised upon the prophecies of Jeremiah. He saw that the time was at hand when God would give his chosen people another trial; and with fasting, humiliation, and prayer, he importuned the God of Heaven in behalf of Israel, in these words: "O Lord, the great and dreadful God, keeping the covenant and mercy to them that love him, and to them that keep his commandments'; we have sinned, and have committed iniquity, and have done wickedly, and have rebelled, even by departing from thy precepts and from thy judgments; neither have we hearkened unto thy servants the prophets, which spake in thy name to our kings, our princes, and our fathers, and to all the people of the land."

Notice these words. Daniel does not proclaim his own fidelity before the Lord. Instead of claiming to be pure and holy, he identifies himself with the really sinful of Israel. The wisdom which God imparted to him was as far superior to the wisdom of the wise men of the world as the light of the sun shining in the heavens at noonday is brighter than the feeblest star. Yet ponder the prayer from the lips of this man so highly favored of Heaven. With deep humiliation, with tears, and with rending of heart, he pleads for himself and for his people. He lays his soul open before God, confessing his own vileness, and acknowledging the Lord's greatness and majesty. What earnestness and fervor characterize his supplications! He is coming nearer and nearer to God. The hand of faith is reached upward to grasp the never-failing promises of the Most High. His soul is wrestling in agony. And he has the evidence that his prayer is heard. He feels that victory is his. If we as a people would pray as Daniel prayed, and wrestle as he wrestled, humbling our souls before God, we should realize as marked answers to our petitions as were granted to Daniel. Hear how he presses his case at the court of "Heaven:—

"O my God, incline thine ear, and hear; open thine eyes, and behold our desolations, and the city which is called by thy name; for we do not present our supplications before thee for our righteousnesses, but for thy great mercies. O Lord, hear; O Lord, forgive; O Lord, hearken and do; defer not, for thine own sake, O my God; for thy city and thy people are called by thy name. And whilst I was speaking and praying, and confessing my sin and the sin of my people,...even the man Gabriel, whom I had seen in the vision at the beginning, being caused to fly swiftly, touched me about the time of the evening oblation."

As Daniel's prayer is going forth, the angel Gabriel comes sweeping down from the heavenly courts, to tell him that his petitions are heard and answered. This mighty angel has been commissioned to give him skill and understanding,—to open before him the mysteries of future ages. Thus, while earnestly seeking to know and understand the truth, Daniel was brought into communion with Heaven's delegated messenger.

The man of God was praying, not for a flight of happy feeling, but for a knowledge of the divine will. And he desired this knowledge, not merely for himself, but for his people. His great burden was for Israel, who were not, in the strictest sense, keeping the law of God. He acknowledges that all their misfortunes have come upon them in consequence of their transgressions of that holy law. He says, "We have sinned, we have done wickedly....Because for our sins and for the iniquities of our fathers, Jerusalem and thy people are become a reproach to all that are about us." They had lost their peculiar, holy character as God's chosen people. "Now therefore, O our God, hear the prayer of thy servant, and his supplications, and cause thy face to shine upon thy sanctuary that is desolate." Daniel's heart turns with intense longing to the desolate sanctuary of God. He knows that its prosperity can be restored only as Israel shall repent of their transgressions of God's law, and become humble, and faithful, and obedient.

In answer to his petition, Daniel received not only the light and truth which he and his people most needed, but a view of the great events of the future, even to the advent of the world's Redeemer. Those who claim to be sanctified, while they have no desire to search the Scriptures, or to wrestle with God in prayer for a clearer understanding of Bible truth, know not what true sanctification is.

All who believe with the heart the word of God will hunger and thirst for a knowledge of his will. God is the author of truth. He enlightens the darkened understanding, and gives to the human mind power to grasp and comprehend the truths which he has revealed.

Daniel talked with God. Heaven was opened before him. But the high honors granted him were the result of humiliation and earnest seeking. He did not think, as do many at the present day, that it is no matter what we believe, if we are only honest, and love Jesus. True love for Jesus will lead to the most close and earnest inquiry as to what is truth. Christ prayed that his disciples might be sanctified through the truth. He who is too indolent to make anxious, prayerful search for truth, will be left to receive errors which shall prove the ruin of his soul. —*Review and Herald*, February 8, 1881

Answers to Prayer

At the time of Gabriel's visit, the prophet Daniel was unable to receive further instruction; but a few years afterward, desiring to know more of subjects not yet fully explained, he again set himself to seek light and wisdom from God. "In those days I Daniel was mourning three full weeks. I ate no pleasant bread, neither came flesh nor wine in my mouth, neither did I anoint myself at all....Then I lifted up mine eyes, and looked, and behold a certain man clothed in linen whose loins were girded with fine gold of Uphaz. His body also was like the beryl, and his face as the appearance of lightning, and his eyes as lamps of fire, and his arms and his feet like in color to polished brass, and the voice of his words like the voice of a multitude."

No less a personage than the Son of God appeared to Daniel. This description is similar to that given by John when Christ was revealed to him upon the Isle of Patmos. Our Lord now comes with another heavenly messenger to teach Daniel what would take place in the latter days. This knowledge was given to Daniel and recorded by inspiration for us upon whom the ends of the world are come.

The great truths revealed by the world's Redeemer are for those who search for truth as for hid treasures. Daniel was an aged man. His life had been passed amid the fascinations of a heathen court, his mind cumbered with the affairs of a great empire; yet he turns aside from all these to afflict his soul before God, and seek a knowledge of the purposes of the Most High. And in response to his supplications, light from the heavenly courts was communicated for those who should live in the latter days. With what earnestness, then, should we seek God, that he may open our understanding to comprehend the truths brought to us from Heaven.

"And I Daniel alone saw the vision ; for the men that were with me saw not the vision; but a great quaking fell upon them, so that they fled to hide themselves....And there remained no strength in me; for my comeliness was turned in me into corruption, and I retained no strength." Such will be the experience of every one who is truly sanctified. The clearer their views of the greatness, glory, and perfection of Christ, the more vividly will they see their own weakness and imperfection. They will have no disposition to claim a sinless character; that which has appeared right and comely in themselves will, in contrast with Christ's purity and glory, appear only as unworthy and corruptible. It is when men are separated from God, when they have very indistinct views of Christ, that they say, "I am sinless; I am sanctified."

Gabriel then appeared to the prophet, and thus addressed him; "O Daniel, a man greatly beloved, understand the words that I speak unto thee, and stand upright; for unto thee am I now sent. And when he had spoken this word unto me, I stood trembling. Then said he unto me, Fear not, Daniel; for from the first day that thou didst set thine heart to understand, and to chasten thyself before thy God, thy words were heard, and I am come for thy words."

What great honor was shown to Daniel by the Majesty of Heaven! He comforts his trembling servant, and assures him that his prayer was heard in Heaven, and that in answer to that fervent petition, the angel Gabriel was sent to affect the heart of the Persian king. The monarch had resisted the impressions of the Spirit of God during the three weeks while Daniel was fasting and praying, but Heaven's Prince, the archangel, Michael, was sent to turn the heart of the stubborn king to take some decided action to answer the prayer of Daniel.

"And when he had spoken such words unto me, I set my face toward the ground, and I became dumb. And behold, one like the similitude of the sons of men touched my lips....And said, O man greatly beloved, fear not: peace be unto thee; be strong, yea, be strong. And when he had spoken unto me, I was strengthened, and said, Let my lord speak; for thou hast strengthened me." So great was the divine glory revealed to Daniel that he could not endure the sight. Then the messenger of Heaven veiled the brightness of his presence and appeared to the prophet as "one like the similitude of the sons of men." By his divine power he strengthened this man of integrity and of faith, to hear the message sent to him from God.

Daniel was a devoted servant of the Most High. His long life was filled up with noble deeds of service for his Master. His purity of character, and unwavering fidelity, are equaled only by his humility of heart and his contrition before God. We repeat, The life of Daniel is an inspired illustration of true sanctification.
—*Review and Herald*, February 8, 1881

Rewards of Obedience

"As for these four children, God gave them knowledge and skill in all learning and wisdom: and Daniel had understanding in all visions and dreams. Now at the end of the days that the king had said he should bring them in, then the prince of the eunuchs brought them in before Nebuchadnezzar. And the king communed with them; and among them all was found none like Daniel, Hananiah, Mishael, and Azariah: therefore stood they before the king. And in all matters of wisdom and understanding, that the king inquired of them, he found them ten times better than all the magicians and astrologers that were in all his realm."

God always honors the right. The most promising youth from all the lands subdued by the great conqueror had been gathered at Babylon; yet among them all, the Hebrew captives were without a rival. The erect form, the elastic step, the fair countenance, the undimmed senses, the untainted breath,—all were so many certificates of good habits, insignia of the nobility with which nature honors those who are obedient to her laws.

During the past three years the youthful Hebrews had been gaining other wisdom than the learning of the Chaldeans; God had been giving them a knowledge of himself. They had placed themselves in right relation to God, and he could trust them with a deep knowledge of eternal truths.

The habits and understanding of the youth who were not instructed by God were in accord with the knowledge that comes from idolatrous practises, and that leaves God out of its reckoning. Daniel and his companions, from the first of their experience in the king's court, were gaining a clearer comprehension, a sounder and more accurate judgment, than all the wise men of the kingdom of Babylon. They placed themselves where God could bless them.

They followed rules of life that would give them strength of intellect and would gain for them the greatest possible benefit from the study of God's Word.

While faithful to his duties in the king's court, Daniel so faithfully maintained his loyalty to God, that God could honor him as his messenger to the Babylonian monarch. It was to Daniel that Nebuchadnezzar, unable to get help from his wise men, turned for an account of his forgotten dream, and an interpretation of it. Daniel and his companions sought the Lord, and to Daniel was revealed the dream and its meaning. And when he had related to the king the vision God had shown him, Nebuchadnezzar said, "Of a truth it is, that your God is a God of gods, and a Lord of kings, and a revealer of secrets, seeing thou couldst reveal this secret."

The history of Daniel and his companions has been recorded on the pages of the Inspired Word for the benefit of the youth in all succeeding ages. What men have done, men may do. If the youth will make the unreserved surrender of the will that Daniel made, God will help them as he helped Daniel. If they will appreciate the opportunities he gives for growing in understanding of him, he will give them wisdom and knowledge, and will fill their hearts with unselfishness. He will put into their minds thoughts that will inspire them with hope and courage as they seek to bring others under the sway of the Prince of Peace. They will have the co-operation of God and the angels. They will work out with carefulness the sum of their salvation, God working in them to will and to do of his good pleasure.

As Daniel studied the Word of God, his understanding became ever clearer; and as he comprehended its ennobling principles, he purposed in his heart to form a character that God could approve. He could not foresee the result of his determination to be true to God in the courts of Babylon; but he resolved that even at the loss of all things, he would preserve his integrity. And the Lord fulfilled to him the word that he has pledged, "Them that honor me I will honor."

There is wonderful encouragement in the story of Daniel for the youth who today are striving to gain knowledge. In his Word the Lord has left his children a divine instructor that will never disappoint those who seek its direction with a sincere heart. Its teachings will give a strength of character and mental development that no other book can impart. Let the student make the Word of God the chief book of study, giving all other branches of learning a secondary place. And as the heart is opened to the entrance of the Word, light from the throne of God will shine into the soul. The Word, cherished in the heart, will yield to the student a treasure of knowledge that is priceless. Its ennobling principles will stamp the character with honesty and truthfulness, temperance and integrity. —*Youth Instructor*, December 31, 1907

Daniel was a moral and intellectual giant; yet he did not reach this pre-eminence all at once and without effort. He was continually seeking for greater knowledge, for higher attainments. Other young men had the same advantages, but they did not, like him, bend all their energies to seek wisdom,—the knowledge of God as revealed in his word and in his works. Daniel was but a youth when he was brought into a heathen court in service to the king of Babylon; and because of his extreme youth when he was exposed to all the temptations of an Eastern court, his noble resistance of wrong and his steadfast adherence to the right, throughout his long career, are the more admirable. His example should be a source of strength to the tried and tempted, even at the present day.

Daniel loved, feared, and obeyed God; yet he did not flee away from the world to avoid its corrupting influence. In the providence of God, he was to be in the world, yet not of the world. With all the temptations and fascinations of court life surrounding him, he stood in the integrity of his soul; for he made God his strength; and he was not forsaken of him in his hour of greatest need.

From the history of Daniel we may learn that a strict compliance with the requirements of God will prove a blessing, not only in the future, immortal life, but also in the present life. Through religious principles, men may triumph over the temptations of Satan and the devices of wicked men, even though it costs them a great sacrifice. What if Daniel had made a compromise with those heathen rulers, and had denied his God? What if, on first entering the court, he had yielded to the pressure of temptation, by eating and drinking as was customary among the Babylonians? That one wrong step would probably have led to others, until, his connection with Heaven being severed, he would have been borne away by the power of temptation. But while he clung to God with unwavering, prayerful trust, he could not be forsaken. The divine protection is pledged to those who thus seek it, and God cannot forget his word.

It was through prayer and adherence to right principles that Daniel was enabled to stand firm in the hour of trial and temptation. The prayer of faith is the great strength of the Christian, and will assuredly prevail against the devices of the hosts of darkness. Satan well knows how needful are meditation and prayer to keep Christ's followers aroused to understand his devices, and resist his temptations; so he tries to lead men to believe that prayer is useless, and but a mere form. If he can divert the mind from these important exercises, so that the soul will not lean for help on the Mighty One, and obtain divine strength to resist his attacks, he knows full well that he has gained a decided advantage.

We are living in the most solemn period of this world's history, when the last conflict between truth and error is raging; and we need courage and firmness for the right, and a prayerful trust in God no less than Daniel did. The destiny of earth's teeming millions is about to be decided; and our own future well-being, and the salvation of other souls, depend upon the course which we pursue. If we possess the same unwavering integrity that characterized the prophet of old, God will be honored through our course, and souls will be saved to shine as stars in the crown of our rejoicing. —*Signs of the Times*, November 4, 1886

Dare to Be A Daniel

All Heaven is interested in our salvation, and I would that our minds were spiritualized, that we might fully realize this great fact. Although Christians will experience trials and difficulties, they should be the happiest people on the earth; for if they are obedient children, they can address God as their Father and Friend. "As a father pitieth his children so the Lord pitieth them that fear him." God has a deep interest in those who are striving to obey his precepts.

Although the children of God may at times be placed in situations that are trying and full of sorrow, they need not imagine that the Lord has forsaken them. Joseph was cast into prison without any provocation, and it seemed that God had forgotten him; but Joseph trusted in the Lord. He had been true to the Lord under temptation, declaring, "How then can I do this great wickedness, and sin against God?"

And the Lord did not forsake him. Heaven gave him wisdom to answer the tempter, and a firm purpose to resist evil. If one of us were called to go through such trial as Joseph endured, would we have borne without complaint and murmuring? He forgot his own trials, and sought to help others. Even in the prison he made himself a necessity and a blessing.

Look at the case of Daniel in Babylon. He was surrounded with all the luxury of the king's court, but he refused to participate in the banquets of extravagance. He would not defile himself with a portion of the king's meat, or take of his wine. When men have the principle that will enable them to stand amid temptation, as did Daniel, the God of heaven will look upon them with approval, and will send them needed help and strength at the moment of their trial. If Daniel had weakly yielded to temptation to indulge appetite, he would have placed himself in a position where he could not have received the wisdom and grace the Lord had for him. He would have brought upon himself physical and mental weakness.

God does not take any man into connection with himself, to give him wisdom and grace, unless he places himself in right relation to the precepts and principles of truth. Man has a work to do to close the door against temptation. He must build a wall around himself, and then God will train his powers for the highest use. It is not possible for us to tell what a man may become, and what he may achieve through the power and grace of Christ. The reason why we are so weak in moral power, is that we are continually venturing on Satan's ground. We should be careful where we go, and see to it that we take no backward steps. For when professed Christians do not live up to the light that God gives them, they can do more harm than open sinners.

When Daniel had been exalted in the court of Babylon, he was not free from trial and temptation. The wise men of the court were filled with envy, and plotted for his destruction.

How earnestly the enemies of Daniel watched for an opportunity to accuse him before the king, but they decided that they could find nothing against him, except in his fidelity to his God. They induced the king to frame a decree, according to the custom of the Medes and Persians, that could not be changed, to the effect that if any man for thirty days offered prayer to anyone except the king, he should be thrown into the den of lions. The king was flattered by this proposition, and as he did not understand the motive that prompted it, he signed the desired decree, and made it a law. Did these men think because they had deceived Darius that they had deceived the Lord also? Daniel knew all about the decree, but when the time came for prayer, "he went into his house; and his windows being open in his chamber toward Jerusalem, he kneeled upon his knees three times a day, and prayed, and gave thanks before his God, as he did aforetime."

The report was quickly carried to the king, and too late he saw that the decree had been proposed and carried into effect through the envy and jealousy of his court. Daniel had determined that he would be true to God. He would let the world know that no king, prince, or power, had a right to come between his soul and God. God did not forsake him, for though he was cast into the den of lions, the angels of heaven were with him, and he suffered no harm. The king, filled with sorrow, spent a restless night in his chamber, and at early light he came to the den, and cried, "O Daniel, servant of the living God, is thy God, whom thou servest continually, able to deliver thee from the lions?" Then Daniel said to the king, "My God hath sent his angel, and hath shut the lions' mouths, that they have not hurt me; forasmuch as before him innocency was found in me; and also before thee, O king, have I done no hurt."

Daniel was soon delivered from the den of lions, and his enemies who had plotted his ruin were themselves destroyed.

Through the trial that was permitted to come upon Daniel, great good resulted to the nation; for it gave opportunity to call the attention of great and small to the fact that God was able and willing to save him who trusted in him. Daniel showed to the nation that Jehovah was a living God. He brought out chapters in his experience showing that God had manifested himself to his servant in a remarkable manner. He told them how he had stood before them as a prophet of the Most High God, and that no earthly power had the right to interfere with a man's personal relation to his God. Thus God was manifested above every king, emperor, or statesman, as the one to be honored and obeyed.

Daniel was counted peculiar, and every man who makes God his counselor, and who seeks him in simplicity of heart, will be counted peculiar by the world. But this is the faith we need, this is the experience that we must have; for Christ has died to redeem us from all iniquity and to purify unto himself a peculiar people, zealous of good works. We should live with an eye single to his glory, and then we shall be able to gain the victory over the world.

We must come out from the world and be separate, if we would be the sons of God, the heirs of heaven. If we do this, we shall enter in through the gates into the city, we shall have a right to the tree of life, and we shall see the King in his beauty. —*Signs of the Times*, November 4, 1889

Every youth needs to cultivate decision. A divided state of the will is a snare, and has been the cause of ruin to many.

In Bunyan's "Pilgrim's Progress" there is a character called Pliable. Youth, shun this character. Those represented by it are very accommodating but they are as a reed shaken by the wind. They possess no will power. Be firm, else you will find your house—your character—built upon a sandy foundation.

Those who would keep in the path cast up for the ransomed of the Lord, must not be swayed in matters of conscience. They must show moral decision, and must not be afraid of being thought singular.

Many there are who are changed by every current. They wait to hear what some one else thinks, and his opinion is often accepted as altogether true. They do not say to the Lord, "Lord, I can not make any decision until I know thy will."If these youth would lean wholly upon God, they would grow strong in his strength.

We are not to fashion ourselves by the world's criterion or after the world's type. "Dare to be a Daniel; dare to stand alone." Thus, as did Moses, you will endure as seeing him who is invisible. A cowardly and silent reserve before evil associates, makes you one with them.

Have courage to do the right. Possess an individuality of your own. If you would succeed in anything that is elevating and ennobling, you must cultivate firmness for the right.

Jesus has revealed to you your value by the price he has paid for your redemption. Your salvation has been purchased with agony and blood. You have everything in your favor. Everything has been done that God could do. In giving Jesus to be the propitiation for your sins, God gave you power to resist and to overcome evil.

You can be resolute if you will. It will require higher help than any human friend can give you, but that help is promised, if you yourself will consent to form new habits. This will require effort on your part, persistent effort; for if Satan sees you taking a step decidedly for Christ, he will employ every ingenious method to deceive and ruin you. But Christ has provided a refuge for the weak and tempted. His angels will help, shield, and guide every trusting soul.

You have within your reach more than finite possibilities. A man, as God applied the term, is a son of God. "Now are we the sons of God, and it doth not yet appear what we shall be: but we know that, when he shall appear, we shall be like him; for we shall see him as he is. And every man that hath this hope in him purifieth himself, even as he is pure." It is your privilege to turn away from that which is cheap and inferior, and rise to a high standard,—to be respected by men and beloved by God.

The religious work which the Lord gives to young men, and to men of all ages, shows his respect for them as his children. He gives them the work of self-government. He calls them to be sharers with him in the great work of redemption and uplifting. As a father takes his son into partnership in his business, so the Lord takes his children into partnership with himself. We are made laborers together with God. Jesus says, "As thou hast sent me into the world, even so have I also sent them into the world." Would you not rather choose to be a child of God than a servant of Satan and sin, having your name registered as an enemy of Christ?

Young men and women need more of the grace of Christ, that they may bring the principles of Christianity into the daily life. The preparation for Christ's coming is a preparation made through Christ for the exercise of our highest qualities. It is the privilege of every youth to make of his character a beautiful structure. But there is a positive need of keeping close to Jesus.

He is our strength and efficiency and power. We can not depend on self for one moment.

Young men and young women, exercise your ability with faithfulness, generously imparting the light that God gives you. Study how best to give to others peace, and light, and truth, and the many rich blessings of heaven. Constantly improve. Keep reaching higher and still higher. It is the ability to put to the tax the powers of mind and body, ever keeping eternal realities in view, that is of value now. Seek the Lord most earnestly, that you may become more and more refined, more spiritually cultured.

However large, however small, your talents, remember that what you have is yours only in trust. Thus God is testing you, giving you opportunity to prove yourself true. To him you are indebted for all your capabilities. To him belong your powers of body, mind, and soul, and for him these powers are to be used. Your time, your influence, your capabilities, your skill,—all must be accounted for to him who gives all. He uses his gifts best who seeks by earnest endeavor to carry out the Lord's great plan for the uplifting of humanity.

Persevere in the work that you have begun, until you gain victory after victory. Educate yourselves for a purpose. Keep in view the highest standard that you may accomplish greater and still greater good, thus reflecting the glory of God.

Daniel and his companions are illustrations of what the young men of today can be. Earnest, whole-souled, these youth would be true to principle at any cost. —*Youth Instructor*, January 25, 1910

During the early years of his captivity, Daniel was passing through an ordeal that was to familiarize him with courtly grandeur, with hypocrisy, and with paganism. A strange school indeed to fit him for a life of sobriety, industry, and faithfulness! And yet he lived uncorrupted by this atmosphere of evil.

To those who will do as these youth did,—close the door to temptation, deny appetite, and place themselves in right relation to God,—the Lord will manifest himself. It is the privilege of the youth today to have principles so firm that the most powerful temptations will not draw them from their allegiance. The company they keep, the principles they adopt, the habits they form, will settle the question of their usefulness in this life, and of their future eternal interests, with a certainty that is infallible.

There is also a lesson for us to learn in the demand the king of Babylon made for perfection in the youth who should stand in his courts. They must be without blemish, well favored, skilful in wisdom, cunning in knowledge, and understanding science. If an idolatrous king should demand such excellence in those who were to stand before him, should not those who have a knowledge of the true God reach perfection of character and capability in his service? Those who expect one day to stand before the throne of the God of gods and Lord of kings, should live each day in such a way that the approval of God can rest upon them. They should seek daily to remove the blemishes in character that lead to sin, and bring into their lives the perfection of character that all must reveal who have a part in the kingdom of heaven.

Character will always be tested. If Christ dwells in us, day by day and year by year, we shall grow into a noble heroism. This is our allotted task, but it can not be accomplished without help from Jesus, without resolute decision, unwavering purpose, continual watchfulness, and unceasing prayer. Each has a personal battle to fight; each must win his way through struggles and discouragements. Those who decline the struggle, lose the strength and joy of victory. No one, not even God, can make our characters noble or our lives useful unless we make the effort necessary on our part. We must put features of beauty into our lives. We must seek to expel the unlovely traits, while God works in us to will and to do of his good pleasure. —*Youth Instructor*, October 29, 1907

What young men and women need is Christian heroism. God's Word declares that he that ruleth his spirit is better than he that taketh a city. To rule the spirit means to keep self under discipline. The youth must not suppose that they can go on living careless and indulgent lives, seeking no preparation for the kingdom of God, and yet in time of trial be able to stand firm for the truth. They need to seek earnestly to bring into their lives the perfection that is seen in the life of the Saviour, so that when Christ shall come, they will be prepared to enter in through the gates into the city of God. God's abounding love and presence in the heart will give the power of self-control, and will mold and fashion the mind and character. The grace of Christ in the life will direct the aims and purposes and capabilities into channels that will give moral and spiritual power—power which the youth will not have to leave in this world, but which they can carry with them into the future life and retain through the eternal ages.—*Youth Instructor*, November 12, 1907

TEACH Services, Inc.
PUBLISHING

We invite you to view the complete
selection of titles we publish at:
www.TEACHServices.com

We encourage you to write us
with your thoughts about this,
or any other book we publish at:
info@TEACHServices.com

TEACH Services' titles may be purchased in
bulk quantities for educational, fund-raising,
business, or promotional use.
bulksales@TEACHServices.com

Finally, if you are interested in seeing
your own book in print, please contact us at:
publishing@TEACHServices.com
We are happy to review your manuscript at no charge.

www.ingramcontent.com/pod-product-compliance
Lightning Source LLC
Chambersburg PA
CBHW070826100426
42813CB00003B/512